Minnow
Strange Happenings

Ray E. Ruoho

Best wishes Bruce
And Jenny,
Ray

ISBN-13: 978-0-578-43000-3

DEDICATION

To Herman Kiland, my principal at Orr High School and my friend,
who helped me along through the years.

TABLE OF CONTENTS

OUR FAMILY ROOTS

My mother and her parents, Jenny and Kalle, and my father's father (Joseph) were originally Finnish citizens. Joseph's wife, Ida, was a first generation American whose roots were also in Finland. Grandfather Joseph arrived in Boston in 1906. My grandfather Kalle (Charles) came to the U.S. in 1915 to establish a base from which to work, and my mother and grandmother, Jenny, arrived five years later. My mother was nine years old at the time of their arrival at Ellis Island, and she had many stories and tales to tell of their life in Finland. She told my sister and me they weren't too happy to have to wait so long for Charlie to get settled so they could join him in America!

Because of the new language, my mother was put into third grade and was very diligent about studying and working for many hours, doing her homework and utilizing after hours school tutoring. She was well liked and had many years of perfect attendance. It didn't bother her, being in classes with classmates younger than she, and she was twenty-one years old when she graduated high school. She had very many friends, became well educated, and mastered the English language while having very little Finnish accent. My mother and father were married on August 23, 1935, and soon after, moved into the home of my grandparents, Joseph and Hilma.

JENNY, ELMA AND KALLE LAMMI 1912

JOSEPH AND HILMA RUOHO 1910

STORY OF A LATE ARRIVAL INTO THIS WORLD

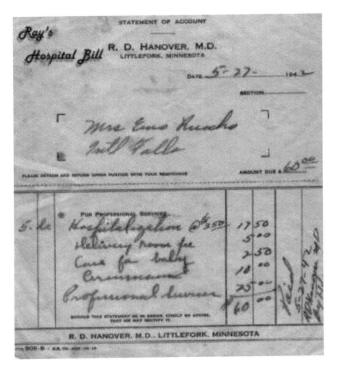

When I was around seven years old, my mother told me the story of me coming late to my post-birth life. There was some concern that I was going to be another problem birth, as two brothers before me had large heads; the first one died when my mother slipped on some ice, triggering a miscarriage, and because the second boy's head was quite large, he was mortally injured during the birth. So, when I was two months later than the expected date, worry began to grow for my mother and father. Thankfully, I was late but healthy with a big head!

My interface with life and memories began when I was two years old. My sister, three years older than I, entertained and pestered me with various faces, noises and words; strange words that made no sense to me at all. My mother said that I would laugh and smile, but when they would speak in Finnish to each other, they would laugh at the strange look on my face. They both tried to teach me to say Finnish words, but I remember not having a clue of understanding. I also remember being in a buggy inside the store (which my mother and father owned) and people coming up to the buggy and looking in and smiling and saying, "how cute" and "looks like his father." I didn't particularly like this, especially when they laughed and said I was "Little Eino." At some point later in time, I remember someone being in our living room at home, making the same statement, and my mother saying not to call me that; I was to be called Ray.

I was a slow starter at learning to talk, though I could understand some of the very basic English. Even so, I had feelings of confusion and my vocabulary was quite minimal. I was well into my third year before sentences were able to form in my mind; simple ones! I took in much of my environment and made sense of almost everything that I took in and analyzed, and I understood feelings and knew when I was the subject of humor. Before I was three years old, I had a baby sitter on several occasions who was very pleasant, kind and lived nearby. One evening, she invited two friends, who were sisters to come over and visit. They were loud and a bit obnoxious, and they smoked cigarettes, which made my eyes sting. As my babysitter was changing my diaper, they came over and watched, making strange faces, laughing and pointing at my physical enhancements. She didn't like their antics and spoke sternly at them to take their cigarettes outside. I didn't see them again for several years, but I always remembered them.

By the end of my third year, during the time when water was running in the ditch from melting snow or light rainfall, I began making dams and creating small ponds in which tadpoles began to multiply. Every day at noon, Ed Erickson, who lived two houses up the road, would walk by and often stopped to talk about my construction progress. One of those times he stopped and asked me what those little things swimming in the water were, and I said, "They look like small minnows." He stooped over for a better look and said, "Those are tadpoles, but they do look something like little minnows, and with you playing in the water every day, you are starting to look like a minnow.

A Mud Minnow; that's what you are, a Mud Minnow!" He laughed a short laugh to himself, turned towards town, and then said again in a louder voice, "That's it, we shall call you Mud Minnow." From that time on, word spread around town that my new nickname was to be "Mud Minnow," which over time became just "Minnow."

I thought it was funny and laughed along with it. It gave me an identity and a place along with many of the other older guys in town who had nicknames. As time passed, I began to learn things that put me in a different category, mainly because I was inquisitive and did things that got me into trouble. I often stayed at home by myself, as both my mother and father worked in their store downtown, and I was not allowed to walk to town even though it was only a few blocks away.

One day after turning four years old, while playing with my toys in the front porch, which faced the street, I spotted a pack of matches on a shelf below a window. I had watched my father many times strike a match across the dark, rough surface and touch the flame to his cigarette. I had never lit a match before, so I decided to try one out to learn how. I tore it from the packet and pushed it across the dark surface, and smoke and fire flared up, burning my fingers a bit and causing me to drop it to the floor. I stepped on it to put it out, then stood there and analyzed what I did wrong, keeping my fingers on the part that lit up. Thinking I knew how to correct the error, I knew what to do next. I pulled another match from the pack and practiced holding it in various ways, moving it across the paper surface first to learn how to keep the flame from burning my fingers. After several dry runs, I knew I had the technique, so I slowly moved another match across the dark surface and got my fingers out of the way soon enough to avoid the flame. When it got closer to my fingers as the match burned downward, I remembered my father blowing on the tip to extinguish the flame. It worked! In my excitement, I lit another one, proving then that I had learned a new skill.

To put my new ability to work, I walked around the porch looking for something to light. There was no paper or anything lying about, but I saw the very thin and light curtains on the windows, so I walked over and touched one. It felt dry and looked like it might burn pretty good. Taking another match, I lit it, held it at the bottom end of the curtain, and slowly moved it upwards until the flame's tip just touched the material. To my amazement and instant shock, the flame at the bottom immediately soared upward and sideways, accelerating rapidly toward the ceiling and sideways to the next curtain (there were eight curtained windows across the entire wall). Within seconds, every curtain on that west wall was aflame – a wall of hot, bright white flame. I was in total shock and immediately realized I was in trouble and had to run downtown to the store and tell my father the house was on fire. I was sure that I was in big time trouble now!

I don't remember seeing any cars when I crossed the main highway, so I guess I lucked out there, and I ran into the store and saw my mother at the cash register. She looked twice at me and promptly said, "You look like a ghost." Loudly I said, "Our house is on fire!" About that time, my father heard my voice and came quickly towards me and asked where, so I told him it was in the front porch. He picked me up and we dashed to the car parked out front. He set me on the front seat, ran around, got in, and we quickly drove to the house. We got out of the car and ran to the front door. When he pulled it open, ribbons of multi-colored smoke greeted us, but there was no fire in sight. However, as we walked into the porch, we saw the blackened ceiling and the curtains, which looked like powdery black spider webs, floating silently toward the growing pile of charred remnants on the floor, like dark flour floating from a strainer! He looked at me and said, "Tell me how this happened." I explained how I found the match book and lit some matches, then touched one to a curtain, and all of a sudden they were all in flames. By that time, my mother had walked in and said, "Did you do this?" My father answered and said, "Our son has learned how to light matches and start fires today. I think you and Ray need to have a talk while I get back to work."

We had a long, long talk. When it was over, I had learned a lot more about fires and the danger of matches burning down the house!

It was a good lesson and I understood every part of it, and I told my mother I would never do that again – not knowing, however, that there might soon be another firebug coming to life with more experiments on the horizon.

In the fall of 1947, at five years old, I was a bit brighter, having learned how to safely light matches, use scissors and walk safely to town, but I still had the disease of needing more input and learning new things first-hand. One day, when my father was working in the store and my mother was inside the house, I took a rake and pulled up a small pile of fallen leaves. While standing there, looking at the pile, I had the bright idea of burning them, as my father sometimes did, so I went inside and found some matches, then went back out to the pile to start a small fire of leaves. Being that the pile was small, I believed it would be safe, so I lit the match and touched it to a dry leaf. The small flame began to smoke a little, and I raked up more leaves onto the small pile, then watched it burn as a small breeze blew the smoke toward the forest behind the house. In one short burst of wind, the fire began to spread, and I realized this was not a controlled fire. As it approached the tree line, I recognized the danger and ran inside and told my mother, "The woods are on fire!" She looked out the back window, and upon seeing the flames nearing the forest, she picked up the phone and called my father at the store and said, "We have a fire in the back yard approaching the forest and we need help fast to put it out."

Within five minutes, about a dozen guys showed up with gunny (potato) sacks, water buckets and a small fire truck. There were guys from the gas stations, restaurants, grocery stores and various other businesses around the village, all prepared to fight a forest fire with shovels, back packs of water with attached pumps, and smoke masks. I stood and watched, not knowing what to do, scared about the fire and about what was going to be another major lecture from my mother and father.

The fire was contained to the ground and within a short period of time, about fifteen or twenty minutes, the fire was out and guys were walking around the area, making sure that nothing on the ground was still smoldering. As they walked back to their vehicles, one by one they passed by me and laughed, cajoled and made jokes that made me feel quite remorseful. Several of the guys I knew from the Phillips 66 station stopped and asked, "Were you practicing how to put out fires or getting experience to determine if you are going to be a fireman when you grow up?" I was glad when they all left, except for the fact that my father was not a happy man; but as usual, he was also not angry and just said, "I hope you learned a lesson you will never repeat again." Sheepishly, I said, "I will never touch a match to anything that could be dangerous again!"

When I walked inside to see my mother, she shook her head and said, "See now what you do. Will you ever learn to not get into trouble?" I learned a lesson that day that put me on the right track for the rest of my life, and I was determined to study activities and conditions to understand what is safe and what isn't. I still make that analysis!

STORY OF JACKIE – EARLY YEARS OF THE MINNOW

Later that spring, in 1946, I was a bit brighter, but still a curious little kid who was interested in everything in my new world. I had this strong need to learn, and I needed input often. My mother watched over me like a hawk, but sometimes she got distracted by other things happening in her life. One day, I saw her scissors and decided I would try them out as I saw her using them; I wanted to learn the technique. When she said I could practice cutting with a piece of paper she gave me, I picked them up and walked around the living room, cutting anything I could get my hands on: string, paper, a piece of cloth. A little later, she was washing the dishes as she did every morning, when, still carrying the scissors, I came upon a lamp cord. The message in my head said, "That looks harder to cut than paper." To prove my thought was correct, I picked up the cord and inserted it into the blades and squeezed the handles as hard as I could. The very large noise startled me as the light from the arc, the bang and the melting blades prompted me to jump backwards onto my butt. I need not explain the reaction from my mother when she saw the melted cutting edges on her best pair of scissors, but the scolding and the scare I got was enough to get the point across that once again, I had done something I shouldn't have.

For the next couple of weeks, I spent more time outside in the front yard, making dams in the spring run-off ditch, behaving myself. As the memory of the scissors faded and the dam project got boring, I decided I needed to take a walk downtown; a walk that I had done several times with my mother since the time I nearly burned down the house. I knew I was confined to the front yard, but with a plan in my mind and a need for new input, I started off for town, which was several blocks away. As a couple of minutes passed, I heard the whistle of a train about a mile or less off in the unknown distance. I didn't know scratch about trains except that they made a lot of noise and moved very fast through town (about 55 mph at the time). We didn't have crossing signals during those days.

As I approached the train track crossing, I saw a young man at the gas station across the street, about 150 feet from the tracks where I stood. He was waving and shouting something I was not able to hear, so I stopped on the tracks and stood watching him as he came running very quickly across the road, up the grade, leaping towards me and swooping his arm around my chest. He lifted me into his arms and ran another twenty feet before sitting me down on his lap on the shoulder of the road. We both watched as the train engine, blowing its horn, and box cars roared loudly past us.

When the noise stopped, he stood me up in front of him and told me how dangerous it was to walk alone downtown, and how the train could have hurt me very badly. Taking me by the hand, we walked back up to my house and he knocked on the door, relaying to my mother the close call at the tracks. After he left, my mother and I sat down in the living room and she gave another lecture about not going places by myself until I was old enough, like Jackie and his sister, Lois, were, and had learned all about the dangers around the village.

Through the years that followed, I recalled the event often. I didn't know his name at the time, but I had seen Jackie around town often, both before and after the train event. Not long after that, my mother told me one day that Jackie was stricken with polio. Jackie, at 16 years old, passed away in 1947. It was a sad time for the village, especially for the family, to lose the nicest, most pleasant young man in town. The funeral service was held in the High School auditorium and the whole mourning village was there, united in grief. It was my first time being filled with sorrow; the person who saved my life was taken away.

MUD MINNOW AT AGE SIX

One day our first-grade class was introduced to Peter Williams - "Pete." His parents were both taken in an accident and he was sent by the midnight train to live with his Aunt Tilly Hoffer at her home in Orr, Minnesota. It was two weeks later that Mrs. Hoffer invited me to come to their home to play with Pete, and after a fun morning, we spent the afternoon in the forest behind the house. This day was number one in social discussion and learning about Pete and his new family, and we discovered we had a similar lifestyle - him with no mom and dad, and I had a mom and dad, but they worked every day. So, Pete and I became instant brothers who were together most of the rest of our days at Orr school, making shacks and tree houses with tin cup communication strings attached. We had Pete's brother "Wiggy" and cousin "Skip," both of whom trained us to hammer nails and do other construction tasks. They also showed us how to make four-wheel wooden push cars with full steering and brakes. Skip showed us how to boil traps, to rid them of smells and organic pieces of old baits, and taught us all about the safety, setting of, and proper locations and positions of traps for musk rats, beaver and other small fur-bearing, four-legged animals, to earn money. We began doing what we'd learned at age 13, the same age that I started to deliver the daily newspaper on a route that also put money in my pocket (not much, but okay). The winter snowfall provided more entertainment for us, and we would build snow huts and tunnels connecting several rooms which we made to be five feet high by shoveling snow drifts into piles.

In the summer we used the boats with motors from the grocery store, and my father bought the gasoline for the cruising of the lake and the river, but when they were rented out to tourists, summer visitors and fishermen, we made our tree houses or took our swimsuits to the beach on Pelican Bay. We had other activities, too, like helping Wiggy and Skip build their own houses. By the time we were 13 years old, we drove cars and had trap lines and a paper route.

In the haying part of the summer I very often helped Gordon Holman, who taught me how to shift gears and drive alongside the hay bales, so he could throw the bales onto the truck bed when I stopped the truck. Gordon also took me along with him when he drove to Duluth to deliver metal scrap to the metal dealers, and I watched him smash cars into flat metal sheets that were about 6'x8' flat, stacked about eight feet high.

During the first freeze in the late fall, we would watch for how thick the ice was, waiting for it to reach 8 to 10 inches or more, assuring it was thick enough to drive on. About once every four to five years, the ice would freeze over with no wind blowing the surface, mirror-slick and thick enough to drive non-stop north to south, one mile across Pelican Bay. Along the way, after previous detailed inspection, we could, at 30+ miles per hour, pull the emergency brake and slightly turn the steering wheel, sending the car spinning in circles for up to a quarter mile if we wanted. We always did a visual verification that there were no crack lifts or clumps of ice to cause a rollover, which we'd never heard of, but the precaution was always required.

There were several years when the "glassed ice" was in place and safe from ice lifts that we put on our skates and tied a sheet to our arms - after night had set in and south winds were present – and with arms raised high, we used the sheet as a sail to propel us at about twenty miles per hour across the bay to visit Basset Point, where the Appleby's home was located. After an hour or so, we would face the hard wind and skate back to town. During winter weekends, we would skate near town where the city plow would clear the snow by the town dock. Sometimes we would spear northern pike in a dark house, about the size of an outhouse with a wood stove.

DELIGHT OF FLIGHT

At age seven, after my first ride in a Piper Cub, I decided I wanted to be a pilot. This was after I wanted to be a fireman, which was prompted by my experiences with matches; the flame-engulfed curtains in the front porch, soot-blackened ceiling and floor, and then nearly setting the woods on fire in our back yard by burning leaves in the front yard (that was the wind's fault). Would I ever learn my lessons?

I found the answers to most of my questions when I was a kid by learning lessons the hard way. My early lessons in an airplane when I was ten years old found me in the place I wanted to be; learning how to fly.

The WWII pilot in our village was a neat and precise man. He really knew how to control the plane and knew about every rule and safety procedure in the air. I got to know Steve Gheen at a young age when my father was taking lessons from him and I got to ride in the back seat of the Piper Cub with pontoons. My father logged in some time, taking about 30 hours of flying lessons, then ran into a time problem of being needed at the store, so he backed out of the pilot plan; consequently, that was the time of the year when Steve was flying many fishermen to lakes near the Canadian border. He invited me to fly with him on his trips to deliver food stuff and supplies, to keep him awake on those flights. It was a good opportunity for me, a ten-year-old interested in flying! Steve explained about the instruments on his front panel and had me read all of his operation booklets over a couple of weeks. Weight and center of gravity interested me most at first, but after that, stalls, turns and landings had my head in the book for more than a month. From age ten to sixteen, I learned how to fly with Steve correcting me as necessary and showing me how to do what he did. By age sixteen, I had a good feel for proper flight.

When I volunteered at age 22 for the draft, I thought there would be more learning involving flight, but by the time that opportunity came along and I was offered a flight back to the U.S. from Vietnam for military planes training, I was embedded with other duties and committed to the other plans I was making for the rest of my life. Returning home, I never again wanted time in the whirly birds. However, by the time I had graduated from Dunwoody, UMD and the U of A, I was ready to take to the sky for further education and experience. I also had a good job and time to spare, and I got my pilot's license with ease.

What a trip! The sky trips were fantastic. On my first solo flight I was caught by an Arizona sidewind upon landing, and it blew the Cessna 150 right off the runway onto the left side, into the tumbleweeds that latched onto my wheel struts. I pushed in the power lever, went airborne again and did a go-around; when I landed and stepped onto the tarmac to clear the tumbleweeds from the wheels, a half dozen onlookers were laughing out loud. My instructor walked up to me and said, "Where in the sky did you pick up those tumbleweeds?"

"Well, sir, it beat me to the runway, then flipped 25 degrees south at 35 knots, and I opted to do a second round."

He replied, "The boys are lined up to give you a gift, pay no attention to them!"

The first fellow to shake my hand said, "Nice landing" and the second fellow took scissors out of his pocket and cut off the necktie someone had put around my neck as I was getting into the plane. Then another guy pulled my shirttail out from my jeans, cut a triangle off and pinned the necktie and triangle to the bulletin board with my name and date and said, "The first solo always gets a congratulations, pilot."

The second solo trip I made was from Tucson to Yuma, and on the way across a mountain range I found a comfortable, brisk breeze so I climbed it over the top and found a tailwind component that allowed me to pull the power back and drift with the wind right to the runway clearance, where the tower called me and had me do a right turn 90 degrees go-around to miss turbulence set up by two F4 Phantoms that passed over me. A close-up view, I thought! But I had good clearance from their wake wind and got a momentary thrill as I watched them take off again at full power. I landed and had my book signed for proof of landing there. On the way back from Yuma, I landed at a small city for a stretch and some water. The trip back to Tucson was great with no stress to deal with.

My training over the next month was in crosswinds, to learn how to hold a straight centerline runway landing every time without fail. It worked well, even through the challenge of a dust devil. My next weekly exercise was how to recover from an out of control dive and then recover from a wingover, both with and without the hood. Because of my practice with Steve, I was quite adept with recovery; I was able to perform on the first attempt, and the instructor asked me how I had already been so accurate, so I told him about flying with a WWII pilot. "Nice flip!"

My third solo trip was from Tucson to Orr, Minnesota to visit with my parents. The first stop along the way was Hutchinson, Kansas and the weather was reported to be clear with moderate winds. When I arrived into the area, the winds were various and crosswinds rough. After having had plenty of crosswinds training, I was not too bothered. The approach control service requested details on my plane (Cessna 172 Skyhawk XP) and my training on crosswinds; I responded that I was well trained and he said I would be in close to limits. I responded, "Thank you, sir, I am coming in!" I set my flaps to about 30%, lined up with the runway center, set RPM's down slightly, hit the first blast of crosswind and bounced ten feet up. I quickly corrected a sudden right wingtip to miss the runway surface, followed by an increase in force to keep the wheels on the tarmac just right and held it there, then

I bounced into a tie down parking spot and quickly secured the ties. I took my papers and instrument calculator and headed to the closest door, pushing it open to the huge noise of applause and some whistles and a voice which said, "Good show, boy, good show." Another voice said, "Was that you bouncing in? Good landing, you handled it just right!" I checked in on my flight plan, took a bathroom and water break, thanked all of them, and took off on my way home.

The trip on my way home to Tucson went well and I laid out a plan to take the whole family of five back to Orr a month later. The plane was still the Skyhawk XP with a ground cruise speed of 150 MPH and it saved us $450 to rent from the flying club in Tucson. We flew that plane even more times, and on the eighth trip I was flying solo to Orr from Gillette, Wyoming. The wind was rough, and I was suddenly hit by a solid downdraft. With the nose of the plane heading straight down, I blasted through a cloud layer and recovered the down fight back to normal level cruise. The rest of the trip was without any unusual or unexpected events.

My job at the time was a very good one, but it was also very demanding and took priority over other pursuits. I decided to hang up the flying for a while, but in the years that followed I hit some health problems that required my attention: high blood pressure, cancer, PTSD and resulting anxiety, and at the same time, the travel bug to spend some time in Finland. It all added up to no more flying for a time. I would like to continue again soon, but today we still are flying with Delta airplanes.

MY FATHER

While my father was living at home in Balsam, Minnesota he was an avid reader and had completed school through the eighth grade. He began home schooling himself in 1928 in any spare time he could muster after all his daily tasks (working in his father's fields, plowing, planting, putting up hay, milking the cows and building numerous piles of rock taken from the fields that previously obstructed the tilling of the land), and he also diligently studied his most favored electronics text books. In the second half of 1928, he traveled to Chicago where he studied music and took a crash course in playing the accordion, becoming very proficient. He kept up his studies until 1930 when he returned to Balsam, where he and several friends formed a small band in the Balsam area. They were doing well up until my father had a rusty hay bale wire puncture that turned into a serious infection, requiring the finger to be amputated. Over the following years he regained some of his skill on the accordion, but not to the level he desired, on account of the lost finger; subsequently, his skill withered and he slowly lost interest and began drinking strong alcohol.

That same year, he enrolled in an electronics correspondence course, studying radio and Ham radio transmitter/receiver theory of circuitry and repair fundamentals, which were prominent at the time, as well as attaining a high level of Morse code proficiency. In 1931 he received his "Certified Radio-Trician" diploma from the National Radio Institute in Washington, D.C.

The early years were tough, but I didn't know how tough until later. My maternal grandfather, Kalle Lammi, had a brother, Herman, who, upon arriving in Minnesota, purchased and operated a grocery store about forty miles southwest of Orr, in the city of Keewatin, Minnesota. He was a very good business man, his store was lucrative, and he could dream about expanding. The major economies those days were driven by the extensive forest areas and large copper mines in and around the

Iron Range, not to forget the well-known Rainy River Lumber Company, which brought in manpower, equipment and supplies from cities south of Orr. Cities like Duluth, the Iron Range cities of Virginia, Hibbing and Grand Rapids, and villages in between all were hiring many immigrant employees from Europe and other countries. Herman saw the beginning of this steady growth and, wanting to share in the profits to be made, sold his store in Keewatin and invested his funds in inexpensive land and stock for the shelves of his new "Lammi's" store in Orr, creating a family gold mine that would continue to prosper for years to follow. Needing employees, and seeing my father and mother unemployed, he enticed them to move to Orr and work at the Lammi store with him and his son, Walter. My father and mother liked the idea of leaving the farm and moving to Orr, so they moved and rented a comfortable home from Herman, who had two rental homes close both to main street and stores.

Upon arrival, both parents had jobs in the Lammi store, but my father soon found out there wasn't enough work to keep him busy, so he took two part-time jobs, pumping gas at the Phillip's 66 station and working the midnight shift at the train station as the night dispatcher. After the second store was up and running in 1943, my father quit his part-time jobs and went back to manage the new store.

Herman's foresight was clear, and he envisioned his niece (my mother) and my father running the new store under the Lammi umbrella. To solidify the deal, Herman provided the up-front money to lease the available building and finish the purchase of necessary stock, storage rooms, walk-in cooler and essential equipment to get the business going; so the deal was made, a family hand-shake company. It was strange for him to fund a competitor, but he didn't give forethought to the possibility that his goodwill was not all going to go directly into his pocket. As it worked out, my father was almost as shrewd as Herman, and with all of the woodsmen coming into town on payday, my father worked out a credit book, so customers could pick up supplies and charge them to an account to be paid later. My father would do the books in the evening, and on the days when the profits were significant, he would walk into the liquor store, where many of the workers were waiting, and slap down a $50 bill on the bar and call out, "TIMBER!" (The purchase of a round of beer for everyone). The book gave him control over who would get a free beer, and if a lumberjack didn't pay his bill or purchase any groceries, he would get a free beer only on the first round. Those whose names were on the positive side would get the rounds until the $50 was consumed! The keg beer was low cost, and it lured many customers into the store. It worked out to be a good method for a long time, as the incoming profit was adequate, and the summertime vacationers and tourists saw a lot of local customers using "Ruoho's store," so they used it, too.

RUOHO'S STORE IN ORR, MINNESOTA

This went on for several years, during which time my father was becoming addicted to alcohol, and Herman had to get his monthly rent check and some profit. My father was still pulling in more profit, but the cost of drinking the booze was accelerating. As a child, I didn't know at the time what was happening, but I did notice that the garage at home developed more hiding places for bottles of whiskey. In seeing this, I created my own hiding places and would tap off about an ounce from each of his bottles into mine. I wasn't addicted, but I never really recognized it at the time to be a problem. I watched closely, so as not to get caught, and I never was suspected, taking less than his normal consumption.

As my mother took over doing the books every evening, she discovered what was taking place, and it wasn't long before the profits began to suffer from the take-off for the kegs. About this time, Herman began to insist on receiving his rent, profit and payoff on the first stock costs. The resulting stress level fell on my mother's shoulders, being that Herman would bring up the subject with her instead of my father, and as time passed, the evening discussions at home became more intense, and the garage stock was costlier, eating up more of the profits and significantly shorting Herman's take. By this time, I had learned a little more of the Finnish language, enough to understand subjects and main disputes and arguments, thanks to my sister Verna's interpretation.

My mother's two strokes and subsequent surgeries took their toll on our home and relationships. The stress levels from the cost of insurance and hospitals reached a point where Father's credit was cancelled, and Mother's medical costs were demanding. Although her health had improved, her living situation had deteriorated. The store was gone, and my father had begun working at one of the iron mines in Virginia, Minnesota.

The level of violence increased, and while she was home, my sister Verna and I held the position of our mother's first line of defense when our father showed up drunk and violent. I had discovered methods to keep him calm and under control, but as the problem continued it became a physical control I was not able to perform, being that he had 80 pounds over me, most of it being muscle. Verna and I made an attempt to jump him once when he was choking our mother, but the outcome was that both of us were thrown to the living room floor; our mother, Verna and I retreated outdoors where mother put snow on her nose, the back of her neck, and on the sides below the ears, and made a hole in the snow drift for pushing the bloody snow in, to cover it up.

By the time I was 18, it had reached the point at which I had to take the challenge, upon seeing him push her onto the bed and put his hands around her neck and start to choke her. Several times she loudly told him to stop and soon, in my fury, my first thought was the 30-30 Marlin in my closet, loaded and ready to go. I dismissed that thought, however, and decided to wait as long as she was still able to breathe and wasn't at the pass-out point. When her noises stopped and I could hear no sounds, I knew it was time to do something.

I believed a sharp knee blow to his left kidney should drop him to the floor, so I quickly got up, ran toward the back of him, and with all the speed and strength I had, propelled my knee into his left kidney. He pulled his hands off my mother's neck and caught himself with his hands on the bed, then turned around and quickly put his hands around my neck, with his eyes like some huge demon or monster glaring wildly into mine as he clamped his tough, large hands into my neck. I knew I was going to be his victim as he lifted and pushed me across the living room floor, down onto an armchair, with my head against the chair back, held strongly by his hands welded onto my throat.

My fists kept trying to hit him in the face, but the angle of his arms blocked every attempt. With a minute passing by and air being blocked, I realized I had just about another minute or less before my strength would be diminishing, and I needed to do something; the only idea that popped into my mind was to extend my right arm as far back as I could and with my fist, swing it fast and hard directly to his left eye. I quickly swung my arm back, and immediately closed my hand to make a fist, and when I did, instead of making a fist, my hand wrapped around the steel reading lamp pole which held the light fixtures and was attached to a heavy steel base. A thought clicked on in my mind with what I could do, and step by step, it was like the pole did the work. My hand swung the pole outward and downward, with gravity assisting and rapidly accelerating its speed. At the bottom of the arc, I pulled it upwards directly to the back of his head, and when it made contact, the shade flew across the room. With about five seconds of delay, he fell from his knees flat to the floor.

My mother had crawled out of bed and was standing by her bedroom door, watching closely and hollering at him to stop, and when he passed out and came to a stop on the floor, she said, "Thank God that lamp was in the right place for you to put your fist around it." "But I didn't know it was even there," I replied. "Then we are really lucky. He could have killed us both! But what do we do now?" I replied, "I have been waiting a long time for an event that would enable us to file papers. This event gives us that opportunity to file and have Gordon put him in jail for a spell and perhaps change this saga."

"What will I do then, I have nowhere to go, and without him, how do I get by?"

Don't worry about that," I replied. "I can make this give you what you have needed for years now, but I need to call Gordon and get him over here before he gets back on his feet and starts it over."

Gordon took my call and I explained what happened and that we needed him to come over right away to prevent any more violence and to file papers. He arrived at our house promptly and took my statement as to what happened, and because mother had difficulty in talking and was very shaky, he asked her if her statement was the same as mine. She nodded her head and said a slightly distinguishable, "Yes."

When I told him that we needed to have him in jail for two or three days and to have someone talk some sense into him, Gordon said, "I can't keep him unless you file the papers," to which I replied, "This has gone on much too long as it is, so give me the papers and I'll fill them out tonight." He said, "I am not able to get them until tomorrow and it has to be on a week day. I can't keep him in jail over two days."

"So, what do we do when you let him out and he comes over here and starts another incident before Monday? This is not a minor risk, and we are not safe. I don't want him on the loose," and Gordon said, "I'll put him in jail tonight and call Judge Loomis in the morning and see if we can extend his incarceration."

Gordon then crouched down and started talking to my father and shook him a bit, and after a few minutes he began to mumble. Gordon started to lift him up on his feet and I offered to help, but he said, "Just open the doors and I can get him outside and into my car."

My mother went back to bed and I took a chair and sat by the bed, and she asked me again, "How are we going to do this?" I told her, "He has just done two chargeable acts of Assault & Battery tonight, an act that is very serious and can be used to put him in a facility like 'Moose Lake' where people go when they cause these kinds of offensives. I can proceed with this in a manner that will have an outcome of treatment for a time that should be able to straighten his head out without you having to worry about how you are going to get by until he gets back. He has never had any jail time, so he will only be there for a couple of weeks and will likely change his mind, acts, and behaviors by discussing what could happen to cause long term treatments and jail time if he does any more dangerous acts. Don't worry about it; he will be in better condition when he gets back."

Gordon, the local constable, locked him up in the jail for several days. Gordon and I previously had talked nearly every evening in the past, and we had parked in front of our house several times before this incident, to hear what was happening inside; he knew exactly what was going on and what my rights were. Gordon told me the next day that he talked with my father several times and said I needed to meet with him, the judge, and my father at the office of the judge on Monday, the next morning, at 9:00 A.M.

That morning, I had the papers and handed them to the judge who read them over and asked Gordon if all of the statements and incidents were correct as stated. Gordon confirmed all the incidents and stated that he personally was there at the time. The judge asked me to explain my problems at home. I described all of what had been going on over the past several years and told him that I was worried, being that I would be gone in two months after school was over, and asked, "Just what are you going to do after I leave? Who is going to look after my mother's safety?" I told him that while I was still home, if anything close to what had just happened were to occur again, I would defend my mother and myself with my rifle if necessary.

His response was, "It sounds like you are planning to kill him."

"No, let me make myself perfectly clear. We have come close to having a death or two at our house at his hands. I have the right of self-defense, and he and you need to know that if he puts me in that position of having to act, like this last time, I will stop him with any appropriate weapon. That is my right. And when I leave, he is under your control, instead of under mine, so you need to figure out how you are going to use the law yourself."

I then took the papers and tore them in half and threw them in the garbage can and said, "My mother asked me to please not have him put in jail for a long time, because she has no other place to go and needs his help to survive." I turned around and walked out.

My father was absent for several weeks, then returned home and quit drinking for a time; no more incidents like this took place after that. The grocery store business then waned to the point of selling out in about 1957, and he finished his working years at a mining company near Virginia, Minnesota and then went to work in a lumber yard in Orr.

MY MOTHER

My mother suffered strokes at a very young age, the first when she was only 38 and the second following about one year later. Her blood pressure was dangerously high, and doctors were scrambling for ideas on how to get it under control. So, during this time frame, my mother was sent to the Mayo Clinic in Rochester, Minnesota and a complete analysis suggested that they cut out a number of nerve branches along the left side of the spinal column. After the surgery was completed, she went through therapy and subsequently transferred back to the hospital in Virginia, Minnesota where she stayed for a couple of months before being sent home with instructions on how to continue home treatments, where I would carefully crawl up and down her back alongside the spinal column to stimulate the nerve bundle to help overall recovery. The doctors said my 50 pounds was just right.

About six months later, my father drove her to Minneapolis University Clinic where they performed the same surgery on the right side. The surgeries were, in total, research studies and the results on the six patients was a failure with only one being successful, and that one was my mother, who within six months was able to walk again, make meals and do much of her enjoyable light tasks and kitchen work. I continued to wash and hang out the clothes and kept the house clean, while she enjoyed sitting in the sun out on the back-porch steps. After several more months, she was able to walk every day with one of the neighbor ladies to get coffee at the restaurant downtown, and she would often say to me, three or four times a week while pointing to the west, "Lake, we go ride in the boat." Her speech, over the years that followed, improved to almost as good as it had been at her previous best, and there was nothing else in the world that she liked better than going on those boat rides. She would sit there on the middle seat with a big smile and happily laugh when the spray from a slightly larger wave would mist gently across her face.

During her 60's, she and my father drove to Florida, where he would work in a lumber yard for the winter and she would visit with many of the neighbor ladies. When they came back to Minnesota for the summer, they visited us in Duluth, Minnesota or Gillette, Wyoming, or wherever we were at the time. They would stay with us for a couple of days or more, and we would drive to their house nearly every month in the summer, to take her fishing or just boating around the lake.

When she turned 70, her blood pressure started going high again. They were still able to come out and visit us, along with Bea's parents, and we would make short day trips to the mountains, Devil's Tower, or just sit around and talk about what we all had been doing. At age 75, she began to lose her memory and also lost words, but she would often raise her arm and say, "Away, away, far away," (while pointing, pointing towards Finland), sometimes with a sort of sad face, but sometimes with a smile, and by the look, we always knew she was thinking about her family home in Finland. We would tell her the story of their home and their trip through the storm on the ocean as they steamed toward Ellis Island; especially about how she helped so many sick people on the ship during the trip and how the crew gave her a "big thanks" going away party for interpreting for them (at age nine), before they landed on the last day. Sometimes when we talked about the stories, she would get a bit teary eyed, but then would again point and say to me with difficulty, "You take papers and go to Finland and see where I lived, and you live in Finland, but you will need to take the papers."

When she was 78, I got a call that she was failing in the Virginia hospital and I needed to fly home. I took a late evening flight from Rapid City, South Dakota to Hibbing, Minnesota and when I got there, she was fast asleep. I sat by her bed holding her hand, and when she woke up and opened her eyes, she got this big grin on her face and said to me, pointing at me while lifting her hand up and down, "You, you, you are an old, old man!!" Her memory had returned, and she remembered me as a little boy; now she could see that years had passed. We both laughed, and the hospital let me take her home, and as the weeks rolled by, her memory began to fade again.

At age 79, comfortably lying in bed, eating breakfast at an old folk's home, she aspirated, coughed, comfortably laid her head on the pillow, closed her eyes and passed away.

She outlived all of the doctors who told her, when she was just 39, that she had only several years left. She had responded to them, "I will dance on your graves!" A good taunt.

In 2011, I took the papers to the Finnish Embassy in California with my papers, applying for a residence permit. Six months later we received the approved permit, and in May of 2012, Bea and I flew to Helsinki. During our six-month stay in Finland we visited multiple times with both Bea's and my numerous second-cousins and our parents' cousins. I often think about how much she wanted to go far away to home and visit with her friends and family. We have met all of them now, and she knew how much we would appreciate them and how significantly pleasant and hospitable they were - as we discovered. Their pleasant greetings and uplifting stories, as we have enjoyed them over the years - our friendly relatives in Finland! We can live there if we desire, but with our immediate families here in the U.S., they need us here until we are gone.

ELMA AND JENNY'S PASSPORT PICTURE

YELLOWSTONE TRIP – 1952

Strange thing!

It is strange that I remember all of this, from so many years ago, and mainly from the only vacation trip we made, somewhere in the early fifties, to Yellowstone and the Black Hills. It was sort of boring until we picked up two hitch hikers, about 21 years old, near the snake pits in South Dakota. They rode with us that day as we drove through the Black Hills and then stayed at a hotel with us overnight. The next day, early morning, we headed into and toured the Yellowstone areas.

With the two of them, the trip was memorably super, and we sang songs, told jokes and talked about many interesting topics and scenery along the road, including the Little Big Horn monument area. They kept me from getting sick by drinking too much seltzer water from the natural springs, and they held me by my arms as I walked on the wooden walkways through the hot springs. After Yellowstone, they continued their trip into Oregon and California while we drove north through Billings and east to Fargo, then home. They sent us a letter a couple weeks later, thanking us again for a wonderful part of their trip.

I have thought about those two guys numerous times in the years gone by. This experience made me reflect on my two brothers that didn't make it past birth. I often wonder what it would have been like if they would have lived, though I know it would have changed most of everything.

On my round-trip hitch hike adventure to Phoenix a week after high school graduation, I relived some of those fantastic days in the fifties.

I wish I would have kept in contact with those two guys, but I was only ten years old.

GILMORE'S ISLAND – 1949

At the age of seven and living close to Pelican Lake, it was essential for me to learn to swim, but my mother and father seldom went to the beach. There were several times the previous summer when my father made attempts to teach me how, but I only learned how to cough up water. The desire was there, but coordination of breathing while swimming didn't happen. I watched the other kids jumping around and splashing water at each other and having fun while I sat in shallow water, picking up and examining pebbles and sand.

In early June 1949, after the ice melted off the lake, my father and I took a boat ride to Gilmore's Island, about 1½ miles from town, where my father was meeting with the caretaker to detail a plan for making changes to the wall structures in the kitchen.

When we arrived at the island, a large black Labrador came running down from the house to greet us. He was exceedingly happy to see someone who would throw the stick (that he dropped at my feet) into the water for him to retrieve, so while my father and the caretaker went inside and sat at the kitchen table, drawing up the changes, the lab and I went back outside and played "fetch" near the house. After a short time, the dog held on to the stick and instead of dropping it, he pulled me down to the end of the dock with it, and then dropped it at my feet. I picked it up and threw it into the lake, and he promptly jumped in, swam out to it, and holding it in his mouth, swam back to shore, raced onto the dock and dropped it at my feet. We did this activity for a long time; then, for variety, I ran to different places along the island's shore and tossed it out. We eventually arrived back at the dock, and when I tossed the stick into the lake I noticed that inside the boathouse was parked a Chriscraft which was tied to metal rings, attached to the inside dock (which was parallel to the outside dock directly on the other side of the wall). I also saw that the inside dock was shorter than the outside dock, made that way to allow the door to close flush with the end of the inside dock. Wanting to see if I could step from the outside dock to the inside dock, I discovered that I could pull myself around the wall by standing on the outer dock, reaching around the end of the wall and pulling on one of the wall studs while swinging onto the inside dock.

At that point, I knew I could take the stick, run to the end of the outside dock, reach around the wall and pull myself onto the inside dock, thinking that the dog would not be able to follow me to the man-door leading out on the house side of the boathouse. Knowing that it would be easy, I pulled myself around to the inside dock. The dog stood there watching on the outside dock, barking at me and obviously trying to determine whether he could jump to the inside dock, a slightly awkward jump of a little over two feet.

When I saw that he was doubtful, I raced through the open outside man-door and peeked around the wall to see him back up, take a short run and easily jump to the inside dock with a very slight slide upon landing on the inside dock. I immediately ran to the end of the outside dock and pulled myself around the wall and onto the inside dock, just in time to see him disappear through the man-door heading to the outside dock; consequently, I raced to catch up with him, but he was faster and when I reached the end of the outside dock, he was already coming around the corner and running towards me. This round robin went on for five or six cycles with the dog barking at me each time before he jumped to the inside dock, where I would be running towards the man-door.

With each time around, I would increase my speed in an attempt to catch him, and he would, likewise, do the same, and bark. I kept going faster and could see him going out the man-door every time, but he was faster on the outdoor dock.

In my overly confident state, I rounded the corner too fast and my grip on the stud slipped; I fell directly into the water about 2 1/2 feet behind the Chriscraft.

The first time I came up flailing and coughing, I heard the dog barking and I looked for something on the boat to grab. All I saw was the exhaust port, about ten inches above the water line, so I decided to lunge for it when I came up the next time; unfortunately, my hand missed the port by several inches.

As I slipped beneath the water, fear set in and words generated in my mind in the form of a clear, tender and distinct voice saying, "You really goofed this time!" I was well into panic and realized I was sinking when the same voice said, "Relax, you will be okay." At that moment, a feeling of relief engulfed me, even though I was going down with my belly and head facing upwards. The light from the sun diffused through the water gave a quasi-mild glow in a wide circle all the way around and above me, which darkened slowly as I drifted downward. About halfway down, another thought popped into my mind, and I wondered if I should try to take a breath. I knew it was not going to help, but in my relaxed state, I took a normal-like breath.

Contrary to what I expected, the incoming water felt soothing, as if air was flowing into my lungs; at the same time, the brightness of the light diminished and there was thick seaweed all around, into which I gently settled at the bottom while the light completed its transition from dim twilight to full darkness.

My last conscious thought was," If this is death, I am with comfort."

My father and the caretaker could hear the dog barking shortly after they started itemizing the project phases and required materials, and they knew the dog and I were having a good time. As they neared the last details, the barking became louder and more intense, and when my father closed the project book, the caretaker commented that the dog rarely displayed such hysterical barking and that they should go down to the lake to see what was going on.

As they approached the boathouse, the dog was anxiously jumping at the end of the outside dock, and after my father looked quickly into the boathouse and did not find me there, he began to look into the water at the end of the outside dock. With the light from the sun now shielded by the boathouse roof, seeing the bottom was difficult, but the dog began aggressively barking and jumped directly to the dock near the back of the Chriscraft. My father followed the dog and laid down on the dock, shielding his eyes near the water. In scanning down, he saw me lying on the bottom…

Feeling like coming out of a dream with no substance, there was a faraway, dull pain not belonging to anyone, just repetitively thudding without hurting. As it continued, a feeling of pressure accompanied the pain and I realized they were both from my back. When I opened my eyes, all was black, but I was aware of water running out from my nose and mouth, and as I began to cough, the pain and solid pressure thumps in my back became unbearable. Gradually I began to sense light, and upon opening my eyes I could see two shoes and water from my mouth falling upon them.

The sharp pain continued, and I finally understood I was being hit repetitively on my back, and the shoes were on my father's feet. My mind began to formulate a sentence, but the water, coughing and pain hindered my voice. Even so, I was able to mutter out, "Stop hitting me," followed by a louder "STOOOP HITTING ME!" The pain impacts stopped, and the dream-state did, too, and I found myself lying on my side spitting, coughing and clearing my lungs!

I had no other words to say, and my breathing was returning to normal. I stood up and the dog came over and licked my hand while my father got a jacket from the bow of our boat. I took off my wet shirt, put on the jacket, and we rode the boat back to the dock by town. With the boat secured onto the trailer, we pulled it home.

Walking into the house, my mother looked at us and, laughing, said, "What have you guys been doing, swimming with your clothes on?" I began to tell her the story of what happened, and my father cut me short saying, "He just fell into the lake and I had to pull him out."

Several months later, I asked him why he kept hitting me on the back, and he said, "I felt that I had to keep the water coming out of you, and all I could think of was that if you were not alive, I would have to go home and tell mother, "We lost another son."

It was a very close call, and we were told that with the ice having recently melted off, being in less than 40 degree water probably slowed all of my body functions down. The hits on the back would have stimulated my heart, and being held upside down hanging by the feet would have supplied blood to my brain while also draining the water from my lungs.

During that time in my life, I was with the teenage fellows often, and when they heard of my incident, they said my swimming lessons would begin when the water warmed adequately. About a month later, five of them took me up to the north dock (called "the big dock") and each of them took me for ten minutes every day for two weeks, after which time I could jump in, dive in and swim with them out to the underwater rock pile about 150 feet or so from the dock.

As for the voice in my head, I have no explanation except that later in life I would be involved with incidents that required more than thoughts and brain power; things that couldn't have been thought of or performed without considerable intervention or tons of luck and coincidence. I believe I'm not alone, and as you will see, taking credit for outcomes of my own doing alone would make the credibility of this book questionable. The voice was there, I swear it, and in the other incidents to come, the same voice was heard, offering solutions. But how, and what entities are for real? In a later story you will read about how a life depended upon my rolling a truck full of wheat over into a dry wash; the voice offered solutions again, very eerie, but real!

SQUARE DANCING AT EVELETH

At age seven, my parents were dancing square dances and I got a significant itch to join them, so my mother began to teach me all the moves associated with the square dance. By the time I went to my second monthly dance, I had learned most of the square movements. It was humorous for most of the elderly ones, so with some variation, their major topics of discussion were about me, dressed in a cowboy outfit - hat and all - doing every move correctly (even though some of the ladies had to bend low and stretch lower). They all thought it was great for a small boy to know so much about the moves. It became my favorite activity in the world and it took my mind off doing things that got me into trouble.

As time went by, my parents' attention swung more into problems with medical health and our dancing slowly came to an end. I was sad on the nights that I knew dancing was happening and I was at home instead. People on the street would stop and ask me why I had quit the dance. The answer was always difficult, but they already knew my mother was becoming ill and my father was having problems keeping the business at the store, with his drinking liquor every evening. I tried to help them both, but I and my sister were of little assistance and the problems began to drizzle upon us from them. By the time I turned nine years old, we had help from families in the village. There was no fixing that could be done by us in our home, so my sister and I gave up and willingly accepted help from our family and friends in Orr.

My dancing was over and was never to resume again.

RED/WHITE DARE DEVILS

During one of the duck hunting seasons, our group of compatriots went to Lammi's north shore cabin and set up our decoys at the west point, one hundred and fifty yards away, and in the early mornings the ducks would fly in and land among the decoys. We often got our limits, but sometimes they weren't flying; on those days we played badminton in the back yard or played cards. The north shore property had a nice cabin and beds for up to five of us.

When the fishing season began in the early spring we often would fish along the shoreline using red and white dare devil hooks. We were at the west point shore one day, casting in our stated areas. Being that I was not having any strikes, I decided I would go towards the cabin, and on the way my mind was concentrating on something in the trees, so I slowed down, not remembering I was about fifteen feet behind Tony, who was casting.

As I walked into his zone, I didn't notice, and Tony also didn't see me. He made a side cast when I was too close, and the hook nailed the right side of my face, right above the right eye, missing my eyeball by about one-half inch and penetrating two of the hooks under the skin; the hook dangled in front of my eye with blood running down my nose, chin and eye.

We put a rag to sop it up at the closed eye and the three of us drove (Tony, age 13, at the wheel) into Orr where Dr. Morcom had his office. We walked in and the doc said, "You boys fishing again, ay?"

He sat me on the table, got his side cutters and clipped off one barb hook that hadn't penetrated my eye lid. Then he pushed another hook from under the skin to the outside, clipped it off and removed the hook. He did the same to the third hook and then bandaged the area. I went home with Dr. Morcom's written instructions and warnings. My mother wasn't happy to see me that way and I received more instructions from her. The following week was when our school pictures were being taken, and the photographer put in his opinions as well; more instructions, but laced with humor.

For a long time after I was called "fishhook." I learned a lot of caution about casting without giving loud and clear boundaries. This incident was clearly my fault by not remembering clear instructions that had been given at the beginning.

This event was an eye-opener, for sure!

I learned a lot on that trip. Another safety lesson, given by my mother, was about observing all things that move in your field of vision; a lesson of analysis of danger. Many of those instructions have stayed with me and have been proven valuable, even when I drive; I scan my field of vision without being distracted. Watch out for anything that moves and might be danger!

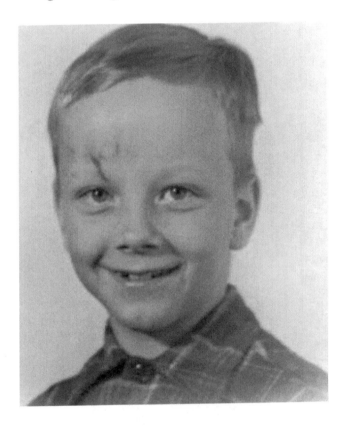

RACE TO THE END OF THE DOCK

In the summer of 1956, I was walking by the Phillips 66 gas station in Orr and glancing down towards the lake, I saw a small boy, about age three or four, who was running as fast as he could towards the dock. As I looked around and saw no one looking for him, I noticed an open car door that looked like it could have been his exit. I took off running as fast as I could down the slope, and when he had reached the dock he was still going full speed. I caught up with him when we were both at the end of the dock, after he had taken his last step and was flying through the air. I swung my right arm out in front of him and he landed right into it.

I swung him around and set him on the dock, then took his hand and started walking back toward the gas station. When I looked up the slope, I saw a fellow calling me and walking rapidly toward us. This was another story I only remembered after my stroke. Later that summer, I had talked with one of the Whiteside boys at a beach party and when I related the story to him and asked who the child may have

been, he said, "The kid would likely have been Little Tom, I believe."
Another accident prevented from the hazard of Pelican Lake.

EARLY EVENING SLEEP WALK

When I was six years old, my mom and my sister were sitting at the kitchen table talking one evening when I sleepwalked into the kitchen, went straight to the garbage can, stepped on the lid lever and proceeded to take a pee into the garbage bag. Much humor and laughing proceeded and I never even woke up. Shortly after, when I was told about it, I recalled the event that I had thought was just a dream. A bit embarrassed, for sure I must say!

BIG FISH HAUL – BENT METAL ROD TO 90 DEGREES

At age 13, when my mother had her first stroke, I was rooming with Ray Appleby's family at Bassett Point. One calm morning I got a rod and reel from the storage shed and took out one of the boats at the dock, riding up the north shoreline to the patch of cat tails where large northern pike fish hang out looking for easy prey. About a hundred feet out from the reeds and tails, I slowly lowered the anchor and started casting to openings clear of weeds, placing the red and white daredevil with a snap to jump the hook to break surface. On about my fifth cast in a shady spot, the jump of the hook was a perfect placement and a large fish tail slapped the water and nailed the hook solid, turned to the side, and pulled and raced away as fast as he could. The drag told me he was about twenty to thirty pounds, and I didn't have a dip net if I could even get him close, so I just kept hauling and pulling and keeping the line taut, not letting him get the sideward pulls. Over the next half hour I managed to get him about eight feet out from the boat; whenever he tried another side pull, I pulled harder than he did and kept working him to the boat. Another half hour later, I had him five feet from the boat when he tried to do a downward pull toward the back of the boat, but instead he came back slowly into view and I got a clear look at him: he was a solid (at least) twenty-five pounds. Largest northern I ever saw!

His last pull was a circle out and I responded by pulling him around, and he began to dive. I hung on as hard as I could. The monster was just short of three feet away when he dove and headed under the boat, pulling on the bending steel rod. When he got just under the boat, his final kick broke the line and I never saw the likes of him again; but did I really get the kidding on this one! For sure I did, especially when they saw the L-shaped rod. The family all said it was their father Ray's favorite rod, but I argued that this was my favorite fish and that I had the best battle of large fish in Pelican Lake, never to be had again... but maybe this year!

THE MESMERIZER

Three of us guys were drifting in a boat one day while rowing across Pelican Bay, and a Mallard came swimming slowly by, so I took out my tremolo and began to play a soft, mellow tune. The quiet melody drew him closer to the boat as he wagged his head from side to side, then slowly lifted a wing and put his head beneath it, lowered the wing and fell asleep! When the three of us began to chuckle, the Mallard quickly drew his head back and flew away. For a period of time afterwards, the guys called me "The Mesmerizer."

DEERSPLAY

One day while deer hunting, a unique event occurred that showed me a bit about the intentions of a deer.

I walked several miles in territory where I had seen deer before, near "Sucker Creek," and I saw a small buck - about two years old - walking up the east ridge. I took a wind test and set my path to keep the wind blowing toward me from where he was walking. As I got closer, being very quiet, I picked up his trail in the snow and followed it slowly; with wind correct and about one-half hour later I found him feeding behind some bushes. I found a nice tree across the trail from where I could watch. Being tired, I decided to rest. At about fifty yards away he became jittery and lifted his head, nose up.

Another twenty minutes had him slowly walking to the trail, toward me. I knew he smelled my presence and was being cautious, but he continued slowly in my direction until he suddenly changed his speed. Now moving towards me at a rapidly increasing pace – an escape pace, you might say – he stayed on the trail, still seemingly aiming at me. I was waiting to see what he was going to do when he arrived, and I was as still as a stick; he was moving quickly, within fifty feet, still barreling forward and closing in fast.

For the last ten seconds, he could fully see me and from his pace of at least twenty miles per hour, he started to set the brakes, all four feet plowing and legs and feet splaying through snow and dead leaves until he reached a full stop and I was focused on his face as he was focused on mine. Now just three feet away, we were very close - eye to eye - both as though we were saying, "Hello, friend!" A full ten seconds of two pairs of eyes staring at each other! No fear. He jumped sideways, and three jumps and ten seconds later, he was gone. Out of sight. "Bye, bye, dear venison!"

BIRDS AND DREAMS AND REALITY

Peter's cousin, Skip, had a Model A vehicle that had the back cut down and replaced with a board rear box for hauling that was often used for firewood, garbage and furniture items, etc. We sometimes used it to set a shotgun over the cab and shoot partridge on old abandoned roads that used to be homestead roads. It was a bit jumpy, but it provided a good view to see the birds perched in trees and eating along the roadside. The old fields were ideal to locate coveys of partridge, but the birds were cautious when we returned too often so we stayed mostly on the old roads and walked the fields. Partridge were the best of eating birds, but seasons were not always fruitful and sometimes over hunted. We had a dozen locations that would always yield a couple or more over several hours.

The old Joker hauled many trips for us and was often another source of income, but over time we got cars and the girls were pleased. So, the Joker was retired and the engine was shot. No more Jokers.

Many years later, I walked the fields and tree lines at my grandfather's 120-acre farm that attracted partridge to feed on the bird seed which we lightly sprinkled. We also saw a salt block he set up by the creek that ran over 100 yards behind his house. Bea and I bought this house, and the fields kept us in good, free food from deer, partridge, fish (from the nearby lake) and beef cattle that we traded with a neighbor for field hay in the late spring and early fall.

Our freezer was always full for winter by fall. Life was easy back then, watching the flocks of ducks and geese, and shooting one or two behind the woodshed feeder annually.

The days went by too fast and our dreams were too big. Isolation sometimes pushed at us, sending wistful thoughts of other places daily in the winter, especially after having to shovel troughs across our road to the highway – every 30 feet – for the 1958 Chevy to push the snow into while gaining access onto the nicely plowed highway.

We gave up the farm and the old farmhouse and sold out to a southern family, then moved on to Duluth, where I completed my education at UMD. Then we moved to Arizona, where I taught electronics and subsequently worked in copper and coal mines for thirty years, where I was tasked with keeping the fleet of large electrical trucks and motors in operable condition; then I retired due to health problems.

Working at mining companies is always a steady job, as there is always something broken down which needs to be repaired, like "right now!" You get somewhat accustomed to this, but it does tend to happen when your health is on the bum, especially in your later years of age when breakdowns at work get you out of bed at midnight after having just worked a 24 hour stretch the previous day and night; or right when you begin opening presents on Christmas morning (for the fourth year in a row, after having been promised the previous year that you would not be called out next year at Christmas), which happened to me five years in a row. My resignation was turned in shortly after that fifth incident.

PARTRIDGE IN THE AIR

Summer had passed, and I was gearing up to take a back road on this first open day of partridge season when the phone rang. It was a good friend looking for something to do, so I told him I would pick him up and we'd go shoot a partridge. We drove near to a spot where there was almost always a bird or two. We got out of the car and began to walk alongside a pile of pulp wood where I had, in a previous year, found a covey of partridge, so I was ready for one or two to take off. About forty feet beyond the pile I heard a sound and chambered a round in my 22 gauge Marlin target rifle, to be ready. Almost immediately, one flew up and I promptly put my peep sight on the front of his chest and squeezed off one round; he fell straight down from the sky about forty feet in front of us, flat out on the ground. Not a single move or flap.

My friend asked, "How did you do that?" My response was, "I have practiced much to know how to sight in the bird and squeeze off the round. It's not difficult if you practice. If you would like, I will help you learn."

My friend did not want to learn, so it never happened for him. I kept hunting birds and not missing much, and I would like to pick it up again if the chance ever comes. Where I really learned how to shoot them was with a friend who made full-size targets by actually drawing them; we then set them up at a gravel pit and shot each target at the same spot on the neck at the same time. It wasn't long before we could hit the target swiftly on signal. It worked! You can get on-target with a 22 gauge because of the speed of the target and by knowing the spot designated by the bird flight path - and by practicing with lots of cans. I had a good season that year in the woods behind our house, and we froze quite a few for the winter, along with fish, beef and deer meat. The birds were many that year, and it was one of the best seasons I ever had. I only missed two out of a dozen or so.

The 22 gauge Marlin target rifle is quite slick and very accurate.

TURKEY SHOOT AT ORR

Every year before Thanksgiving we attended the annual target expert day. Nearly every local business posted a list, and each list had space for ten shooters; you could sign up on as many lists as desired. My Marlin rifle was a 22 gauge with long rifle bullets and a peep site, and the bullets were hand-loaded by our local gunsmith for accuracy; it certainly was that. My first year in shooting, at age fourteen, I won two turkeys, and the following year I walked away with four. Shooters were coming to town from miles around with high velocity rifles, but I still took more turkeys than any of the other best shots. The next year, the city board approached me with a request that I not attend the shoot because the out-of-town contestants spent a lot of money in town and didn't like to lose to a kid. It was to be my last year anyway, so I walked the fields and shot partridges on the fly – more fun than shooting three rounds into a dime-sized circle on a square target. The birds tasted better than a turkey, anyway, roasted with stuffing!

DUCK HUNTING

When duck season began back in those days, we would plan our days and our hunting locations. Our choices were varied by selection of beaver dams, rivers and lakes. The prime choice was often the Nett Lake Boise Forte Reservation. There were years when the northern flight would arrive in flocks of hundreds at a time. We would get up very early, like 4:30 AM, and arrive at our school friend's home with ammunition for him so that we could be setting out our decoys by 7:00 AM. The flocks flew all around the lake in search of their favorite locations of natural wild rice growth. By 8:30 AM shotguns were heard all around the lake and the three of us, who were all good shooters, had our take early. Our count going back home was limited, so we left the majority with our friends on the reservation as they had no limits. We always had enough anyway, mainly bluebills and mallards; the best eating ducks when stuffed with wild rice.

These days were often not very long, being that hits were many, and our trip back home was in the early afternoon which gave us time to clean and prepare our take for dinner, and to freeze the remainder.

The northern flight was not always very big, but on those special years when the flocks were huge, there was much celebration and the fun was long enjoyed by all. Back to school, the days that followed were full of gaiety, jokes and inflated stories about our own – and others' – takes. Life was good those days, but not so when ice was on the lake and we had to break it with our paddles to create a scene to entice the ducks to fly in, or just fly by, so we could take a few shots. There were some seasons when we were able to make several trips, regardless of the condition of the ice on the lake, and we would head for the river to fish or quietly stalk and surround a beaver dam. Great days they were!

DOUBLE BARREL SHOTGUN

It wasn't that we weren't safe all the time (well, maybe just part of the time). One of the days when the ducks weren't flying, we were in the back yard with my double barrel shotgun and one of our group wanted to see what kind of pattern the double barrel made, so we set up a cardboard box at 50 feet away. I explained to our curious friend that the double barrel 12 gauge has a trigger pull sequence that absolutely has to be followed or both barrels will fire at the same time and give a very solid kick-back, and that my gun had both barrels loaded with special magnum power-load (usually loaded for geese). If you pull the back trigger first, both barrels will fire, so you must pull the front trigger first.

"Do you understand this safety fact must be followed – front trigger first?"

The answer was, "Yes, of course, I am ready to do that!" With that, he took the gun in hand, put it to his shoulder, and after several seconds he did, on purpose or not, pull the back trigger, and the results were as follows: 1) The fore-stock fell straight to the ground. 2) Both barrels fired as we'd said they would, and the twin barrel fell straight to the ground. 3) The rear stock split in half, one half flew off to the side and landed on the ground and the other half flew to the rear, rapidly propelling our soon-to-be ex-group member who flew straight back – six feet – and landed flat on his butt with a look on his face that I had never seen before. 4) The box flew 25 feet into the trees. After a long silence, his spoken words were "Wow! As you said. Speechless!" The group watching the show got on his case for not doing as told, and I was startled as I had never used the magnum ammo for two barrels. Once I did fire it with two barrels, but with standard duck load, causing no damage. Now we knew the damage would be so powerful that we were all stunned for sure!

We all shared the dangerous event and the safety issue we had witnessed. I took the pieces to our local gunsmith who fixed the trigger problem and located new parts. The shotgun is still in use, working well and safe!

ANOTHER MALFUNCTION: ANOTHER SHOTGUN

Another early day, we left to set up decoys and to put them in the water before the ducks set about looking for a landing place. The boat was a rowboat, so three of us took our positions and the fourth, middle man rowed us along the shoreline to where the decoys would be placed. As we approached the drop point, we spotted several small flocks of three to six ducks each, and we quickly set the decoys in place. Two of us loaded rounds as one of the smaller flocks was coming in low, to land. Someone pointed out that we might get a shot, so a third member of our hunting party quickly chambered a round and pushed the bolt in, but with a faulty firing pin and safety assembly in place. The bolt closed and with the pressure applied, the pin fired the round and the shot of the round went off directly into and through the bottom of the boat. Instantly water was spouting up into the boat, the ducks flew away, and the man on the oars was cussing loudly and rowing hard toward the dock, a hundred yards away, while two of us bailed water with one coffee can.

The water was flowing in quite a bit faster than we could bail it out, so we increased our cycle speed with the can and reached a point closer to where the incoming water equaled the bailout water, and when we got to the dock, we pulled the boat ashore and tipped it over, dumping out about one foot of water. Cousin Tony, the owner of the boat, was still quite upset over the incident and as a result, Oscar George – the caretaker – came out of his shack and asked the cabin owner's son what had happened. The answer was very blunt and loud and full of cuss words for a moment, as he pointed out the damage, but George said, "Boys, boys, we do not panic, boys. We can fix this just like new again! You wait here, and we fix!"

Oscar went inside his shack and came out with a handful of tools: A rasp, a hammer, several sandpaper sheets, a saw, a small can of marine glue, a can of paint the same color as the boat, a small can of thinner and a tape measure. He set them on the dock and walked behind the shack, and he came back with a dry branch. He measured the diameter of the hole in the boat, then cut and fashioned a plug from the branch to fit tightly into the hole. He put glue on the plug and inside the hole and lightly hammered the plug flush into place, then he said, "Now we wait boys, till glue sets. So, go into cabin. We all need coffee!"

We all gathered in the cabin and discussed the malfunction incident, and Pete told us the shotgun was recently purchased by his cousin and was not test-fired, and that he would have it repaired at the gunsmith's shop, which he later did. Another safety item repaired!

Oscar George led us back to the boat, and we watched as he filed and sanded down the plug and hole edges to match the boat bottom and then thinned the paint to be absorbed into the matched wood. By the time we left, several hours later, we looked at the fix and it was a perfect match. Oscar grinned and said, "Nobody know the hole was ever there!"

I visited with Oscar at an old folk's place north of Duluth, quite a few years later; the Lammi family had paid the way for his remaining years. He passed away in peace. Good old Oscar!

PARTRIDGE ATTACK

One day as I was walking on a trail to a ridge overlooking Sandpoint Lake, where you can stand above the lake which is 50 feet below, I watched kids dive from it – something I wouldn't want to try. Another day while walking the trail, I heard the full sound of a partridge beating on a log to protect its little ones. Twenty feet further down the trail, the partridge exposed herself mid-air, scaring me with her wings beating the air and causing a major wind storm right in front of my face. For twenty seconds she flew up and then down to the ground, with full wing span in my face, telling me to go away. Scary! I would rather look into the face of the deer!

PERIL ON PELICAN – PELICAN LAKE TRAPPING

During the winters of 1954 through 1958, my friend Pete and I had two trap lines on Pelican Lake; one going north from town, the other going south. Every morning before school we were up at 4:30 AM and on the lake by 5:00. The odd number days had us taking the north line, even number days the south. On the good weather days, we were back at the house by 6:00 AM, and on bad weather days, by 7:00. We cleaned up and finished breakfast shortly before the bell rang at 8:00 AM. We would leave the muskrat and/or mink we had caught behind the garage, and after school, Pete and I would build a fire in the garage wood stove, then skin and stretch them. At 5:00 PM I would go to the bus depot and pick up my newspapers to deliver, and I would be back home shortly before 8:00 PM (usually!). On days when the snow was deep, it took a little longer, but it didn't slow us down much, as Pete would take the second paper sack and we each did one half of the route. We started the trapping and paper route routine at age thirteen and our last season was at age seventeen, after we met girls who were not impressed by a couple of smelly boys. A lot of stories evolved from our antics.

During those years, we had outside temperatures in the -10's to -40's, and we almost always had two weeks or more where the -40's stretched to -50's and the blizzards would close the school for up to a week at a time. We enjoyed the days off, as the heavy snow was demanding, and we needed a rest from our routine.

The heavy snow also created additional risk, as the cover over the lake and river would occasionally insulate on the top of the ice. The moving water underneath the ice, some being underground spring flows, would melt the ice 8 to 10 inches from bottom to top, leaving an opening in the ice under the snow that was not visible until the warmer temperatures arrived to melt the snow.

Two days before our last day of trapping happened to be the river trap line day, a day following a nighttime snowfall of about four or five inches through which we left our footprints as we made the round: Down the east side, cross the river and back up toward town on the west side, then across at the mouth of the river and back to town.

The next day was the north trap line checks. The day after that, when we reached the river crossing point for the last time, the footprints we had left in the snow two days earlier gave us the shivers, as halfway across was an oval 6 feet long by 4 feet wide of open water, with our tracks in the snow on both sides of the opening. The running water below had melted a potential accident! That was our last day of running traps on Pelican. On the down waterflow end of the open water was a small tree, and I had dreams over 20 times of being under water, looking at the underwater growth. I can remember the details clearly, that perfectly could have been real, had we gone under!

BEEB FALLS THROUGH THE ICE: EARLY SPRING, 1953

About two weeks after that, with the beginning signs of spring and the ice still about ten inches thick, Tony, David Johnson and I were skating on an area near the city dock that was plowed off every winter for skating. We had been skating for about an hour, and as we were sitting on a snow bank near the dock talking, we saw my neighbor, Walter Gabrielson, Jr. (Beeb). Beeb was leaving an area about 150 yards away where he, his father and another helper were cutting blocks of ice from the lake that they would haul to an ice house, to be used by a gas station where fish were prepared for shipping during the summer months. We watched him start jogging toward the skating rink while the other two men continued working.

As we were talking, I stood up and asked when we would meet back here again, and while David began responding with an answer, I had this dark feeling of imminent doom – the same feeling I had upon falling off the dock on Gilmore's Island. My first thought was Beeb, and when I turned to see where he was, I saw nothing except his tracks leading toward the snow bank surrounding the skating area. I yelled loudly and said, "Hey, Beeb isn't there. Something must be wrong. I'm going over there to see what the problem is. He must have fallen."

I skated as fast as I could to the snow bank, and as I arrived, I saw Beeb trying to pull himself up onto the ice and then sink back down into the icy water. He looked up at me with fear in his eyes and reached his hand up toward me. In a hoarse, panicked voice he was saying," Help me!"

I crawled up the bank on hands and knees, thinking "How am I going to get him out of there?" When I reached the top of the bank, I wasn't near enough to come close to taking his hand, so I pushed myself downwards toward him, stretched my arm out and extended my fingers. When he lunged in an attempt to grab my hand, and his fingers came very close to mine, I realized that if he did take my hand, I would be pulled into the hole where he was thrashing. I quickly backed off and jumped down off the bank to the skating area and said, "Hang on Beeb. I'm going to skate as fast as I can to get Tony and David over here. I'll be back with them in just a minute; we'll get you out of there. Hang on!"

I quickly skated to where they were just starting to unlace their skates and I hollered, "Lace those skates back up; we have to get Beeb out of the water. He's fallen through the ice! LET'S GO RIGHT NOW!"

I raced back, and as I went, I did a quick scan of the back of the Legion Hall, where there was scrap lumber from time to time, but there was nothing there. I turned around and looked toward Tony and David, shouted again for them to hurry, and then turning to Beeb said, "They're coming now. We'll have you out of there in a minute. Hold on." Having said that, I looked again to see if there was anything we could use to hoist him out. Beeb was no small fellow, a good 180 pounds and just under six feet tall, so we were going to need a plan to jerk him out.

While looking at Beeb and the snow bank again, a plan momentarily formed in my mind: Tony and David would have to go over the top of the bank like I did, leaving a space between them. I would then lay on my back in that space between them, with my head downward toward the skating rink. In that position, with my knees up and my skate runners firmly planted in the snow bank, I would lock my arms around their ankles. Then, when Tony and David each had tightly grasped a wrist, I would count to three, followed by a loud "PULL," then straighten my legs to push myself down the bank toward the skating surface, with my arms locked around their ankles, and the three of us would propel him directly out of the water.

So, as Tony and David skidded to a stop, the plan in my mind was complete, and I laid them out side by side, with just enough room in between them for me to lay on my back, head down and knees pulled up, skates in the bank, ready to begin. I told them, loud enough so Beeb would hear, "Scoot down just far enough so you each can very tightly grab a wrist, and then loudly tell me that you're ready."

When they both had given me the shout that they had him by the wrist, I loudly yelled that I will count to three and holler "PULL." Upon the count of three, I shouted as loud as I could, "PULL!" and we popped Beeb directly out of the hole. I hung onto their legs as tightly as I could, knowing Beeb would be pulling their arms to start his fast exit up the bank; within just moments, I saw Beeb storming over the top of Tony on my right. In another several seconds, Tony rolled upwards and on hands and knees, rapidly crawled up the bank. David on the left did the same, and a few seconds later, the four of us were standing in a circle on solid ice, facing each other. Beeb, shaking and shivering, was the first to speak, saying, "Th..Th..Th..Th… Thanks boys! I need to get home fast!"

I asked, "Do you want me to run with you in case you need help?" His response was, "Nnn..No. I'm okay now." We watched him in silence as he ran to his house several blocks away. Another close call adding to the perils of Pelican Lake!

JACK BURNSIDE

One year after Walter Gabrielson fell through the ice, Jack Burnside, while crossing Pelican Bay a couple hundred yards north of where Pete and I had the close call, fell through the ice. Pete and I were at my house at the time, about 8:00 PM, after dark, when we heard a very loud hollering coming from the bay. We walked down to the dock in town where several other people were gathered, and they knew who it was, but nothing could be done, as there was no way anyone could get to him. The precariously layered ice was still on the lake, and he had unfortunately fallen through one of those open yet unseen melted areas. Having no lightweight aluminum canoe at hand, a quick rescue was not an option. Another sad time on Pelican Lake. Jack was a very good worker, the best in town, I'm sorry for the family still.

Several years later, a father from Virginia, Minnesota and two of his children were riding on a snowmobile and fell through another opening beneath the snow at Patten's Point, about a mile across the bay from the Orr dock. Too many sad stories for the family and the village.

57 FORD 500

The red and white 57 Ford Fairlane 500 with dual spotlights was a piece of art, along with being a head-turner and a sure date – a car of beauty that magnetized two-legged beauties with a smile. Its effect was similar to that of the red and white daredevil casting lure on an active hook for Northern Pike when fishing among the weeds along the shoreline on Pelican Lake. A hit on every cast!

What else can I say about an eye-catcher? The likes of a diamond of diamonds that is so precise it needs to be kept under lock and key, but then the 500 wasn't a gem to be hidden away when it invited a line-up on the street, waiting for the next ride; I ramble too much. How else can I describe this gem that treated me well over five years of pleasant travels and was known by many in the cities of Minneapolis, Virginia, Duluth and Cook, Minnesota?

But alas! Many good things in life wither or rust away, and in this case the demise was a burial of five feet of overburden. I was in Vietnam at the time, dreaming of being home again, driving my girl around town and planning our lives; when I arrived home to start living those dreams, I had to do so without this gem in my garage.

It was a shock to find it gone, but I had no money to bring it back to the beauty it was. Now it takes a memory and a photograph to bring it back to life. This car reminds me of my first and favorite blue guitar that was stolen from a friend who borrowed it for a few days. I guess I will just hang another picture on the wall with Bea and the guitar and the car; Bea is sitting on the front driver's side. I don't have a picture of the 410 shotgun that also was stolen, from behind the seat in my pickup at a small, remote lake frequented by mallard ducks because of the wild rice – their favorite meal. I learned to lock doors the hard way after fixing the locks and keeping things of value out of sight. It could have been worse if they had found the truck key I hid under the passenger seat in an empty, beat up cigar box wrapped in an oil-checking t-shirt rag. I think I have learned my lessons well again.

Now I drive a 2015 red GMC Volt hybrid. Not as attractive as the Ford 500, but I traded a car whose miles per gallon was terrible compared to the Volt, which cost a pocket-full more dollars but gets an average of over 80 miles per gallon (which almost covers the car's payments). Good deal!

57 FORD

HERMAN KILAND... #1 FRIEND

School principal Herman Kiland was a friend and mentor to many students needing help, and I was one of those kids. With my mother having high blood pressure and strokes while my father was tied up in the grocery store with long hours and trips to Duluth to restock the goods, my sister and I were held back to keep up with everything needing to be done at home.

Father's troubles stemmed much from alcohol, and after an evening at the local liquor store he was often violent. During these nights, when teachers and principal Kiland walked by, they heard the arguments and saw my sister and me sitting under the weeping willow tree in the front yard, smoking cigarettes and staying clear of his loud, threatening voice.

After Mr. Kiland witnessed these situations, he would call me into his office the following day to discuss my school work and to help pick up my self-image and my grades.

After one loud and violent evening, he called me into his office and said he wanted to have us over for an evening dinner at his home, to help our dilemma. He gave us an invitation and a specific night and time. I passed this on to my mother and father, though I had doubts if father would be able to make it; and I was somewhat right. After two calls to the liquor store on that early evening, I convinced them to send him home for our dinner with the Kilands. An hour later, he walked into the house; well, he could hardly walk.

I called Mr. Kiland and let him know the situation, and he said, "Bring him along anyway." So, we did. He was doing somewhat okay until the food was set on the table: nice steaks, potatoes and gravy and vegetables. Everything looked great! Then my father ate a bite of the steak and loudly demanded, "Salt!" and it was passed to him. He picked it up, shook it, and set it down, then passed out with his face flopping right into the mashed potatoes! I looked at Mr. Kiland who quietly said, "That's okay, we will take him home after we finish our dinner," which they did.

Mr. Kiland drove him home two hours later and helped him to the couch and laid him down on it before he passed out again.

The following Monday at school, Mr. Kiland called me to his office in the morning, and I walked in and said, "I really am sorry about that and don't know what to say." He said, "That's okay. I should have known. I will stay out of your problem and sooner or later, the tide will turn. Keep working well as you are in your classes. Several teachers have said your progress has been very good over the past weeks, so keep it up."

As he had said, "sooner or later" the tide did turn. One night my father's violent actions changed his temperament for the rest of his life.

BIKE HIT BY CAR

Not long after having made enough money on my paper route to buy a new Schwinn bicycle, it arrived at the post office and two of us carried it back to my home and assembled it, then went on a three-mile test to confirm that this new bicycle was everything it should be.

One day the following month I was riding at a good speed and heading toward the main street in town. I approached the highway and looked both ways for oncoming cars, and I saw no vehicles in either direction, but long pulpwood trucks were lined up blocking the view to the south. I began to cross the road when a fast-moving car hit the back of my bicycle and I flew straight forward, landing flat on my back on the blacktop, sliding atop the coarse gravel with my head bouncing, driving pebbles under my scalp and through the back of my shirt and peeling skin off seven of my vertebrae.

I slid to a stop as I came up a rising bank. Several local guys saw the whole event and I was taken to a clinic seventeen miles south, and I woke up that evening wrapped with gauze and tape with a doctor looking into my eyes, waving his hands. My mother and father were sitting in chairs nearby, watching and talking with the doctor. I asked, "What is the problem?" and the doctor gave me a mirror to see my wrappings. He said, "You had a collision with a fast-moving car and landed on a batch of coarse gravel, so here you are. You have a concussion and we will need to hold you here for a couple more hours to further check your symptoms. As you see, your mom and dad will be here when you have been released." My father stepped in saying, "Your bike went flying and didn't land on wheels! You won't be riding that bike anymore, but better it was the bike than you — even though you now have some rocks under your scalp, or should we say, rocks in your head. Ha ha ha!"

The doctor stepped in and said, "You need to be quiet now, for another hour or more, and your parents will slip out for a meal at the café. So far, you are coming out of your concussion. You're doing good!"

Later the doctor came back and gave my father a list of what I should be doing for two days of healing time. More questions and answers took a short time and then he told my parents it was okay to go home.

The healing went well, but the worst part of it was that forever, as my sister told me, I had rocks in my head!

The driver of the car didn't stop at the scene, but license plate numbers were taken. Several minutes later the driver, feeling bad at not stopping immediately, returned to the scene. My father made a deal and talked with the guy several times on the phone, and he paid the hospital and doctor fees, the cost of the bike, and several hundred dollars to settle the issue, with no legal charges applied.

I never saw the money from the driver. I took out my old bike and used it for the next few years until I no longer needed it.

Over the many years that followed, the rocks in my head worked their way to the surface and my sister gave up her taunting. Good ending!

31 CHEVY

Hi, Dolly! The answer to your question is not a short one, but I will attempt to boil it down somewhat. The longer version is still in process...

The 31 Chevy was the first car Pete and I had. We bought it at age 13 for $25, earned from my paper route money and some of our trapping income. It was in nice condition and had been stored in a shed for a long time. We had to have the Babbitt bearings checked out, so Pete's cousin Skip showed us how to do the job. We fixed up the tires, cleaned it up and painted it black with yellow trim, white paint for the white-wall tires, of course, and bright yellow for the wire spokes – all colors being good quality automotive paint from my dad's garage. We painted it in the garage and let it sit for over a week to cure. After we drove it for a month or so, we gave it a good polish job, and you could see your face in the shine of the black. Then began our road trips, including the back road through Buyck to Cook and all back roads N,S,E & W heading out from Orr. We used it when we were trapping, hunting, fishing, and for just about anything else we could think of. It was a nice little car, and the rumble seat had never been sat in before we bought it!

The night of the Wiggy's wedding (Pete's brother William), we all got somewhat tanked up, and I had to go home from the Legion party around 10:00 P.M. to briefly check on my mom. On the way, I saw two people by the car where we parked it at the Lutheran church. I walked down to where they were and saw that it was two local guys. They were searching for the key and asked me where we had hidden it. I told them I didn't know, but they didn't believe me and continued to look. It was up on the back-window ledge under some papers, and they soon found it. They talked me into going with them for "just a short ride" up the Murtle Lake Road. I didn't want to go, but they persisted, and I decided it was better to go with them, to make sure they came back with the car. We started on the short drive and turned around several miles up the road. On the way back, Jenk pulled into a farm road and stopped. He told me to drive, and as I knew I was in no condition to drive, I refused. After being badgered to do so, I got out and unsteadily walked around the front and got into the driver's seat. At that point, I was aware of being somewhat visually impaired and said I was unable to drive. After several statements back and forth, I shifted into low gear, floored the accelerator, popped the clutch and steered the car down through the ditch and through the fence, pulling down a hundred feet or so of wire as we bolted out into the field. I did a couple of fast laps around the field and then drove back through the fence, hit a fence post, backed up and again drove through the wire, pulling it and the fence post along behind, through the ditch and onto the road. There I stopped and sat watching out the front window at the steam rolling up from the radiator and engine compartment. The two boys promptly got out and said they were leaving. I sat there for several minutes trying to figure out what happened, then got out, leaving the car right where I stopped, and proceeded in a daze to walk back to the Legion Hall. For many years after, I was totally unaware of anything that had happened that night, except an older lady giving me the nickname Doc Ruoho. She had seen me earlier that night by the lake behind the Legion Hall, helping a couple of young guys who had too much to drink and were suffering the effects of the worst kind.

Pete and I talked about the demise of the car many times after that night, but I remembered nothing of the event until 2001, during a time in which many suppressed memories of my youth began to return; memories of things I did while growing up, intoxicated, or in Vietnam. Most of those memories had been totally hidden away, locked back in the forbidden cubes of gray matter, waiting for the opportunity to slip out to the present.

Many more events have surfaced since my stroke in 2009, things I continue to add to my list of writings. Sometimes I wish the recall process had never started, as it is not the life story I otherwise would have told. It gives new meaning to "the truth hurts."

The 31 Chevy story was just one in this long list of bad memories. I still have small glitches of scenes past that recur periodically, things that I have not as yet had enough dream substance to recognize or connect details of the events. Over time, however, occasional pieces begin to fit together, stimulating continuity of a forming story. I have been writing about these as they grow into larger scenes, finding that it prompts more of them to slip out from their dark isolation, in measured quantities, perhaps as I am ready to deal with them, like the 31 Chevy. Consequently, my mind is slowly reconstructing my past life with reality events in sequences as they really happened... Unpleasant, but true.

I quit drinking the first time when I was 21 years old, on May 22, 1963, two days before joining a combine crew heading out on the summer grain harvest. The second time was the day after leaving Vietnam, February 10th, 1966 when, in the absence of varied stressful stimuli, I recognized that many more internal repairs were needed to become the person I always wanted to be.

So, to answer your question, Dolly, the 31 Chevy incident was one of many symbolic forms of rebellion in my youth. It was a time of being overwhelmed by conflicting environments and the inability to deal with too many problems which wound up ruling my attitude and actions. The Chevy and liquor were parts of many suppressed events that served initially as a retreat from reality, offering an escape from the conflicts and providing a psychological disconnect.

BEAR'S NIGHT

Pete and I that year had a summer plan that included camping overnight at the beach at Patton's Point. After swimming for several hours, we ate the lunch meat sandwiches that we had packed for dinner and sat in our tent until dark, then crawled into our sleeping bags.

About an hour later, still not asleep, we heard some rattling noises outside. I opened the door flap of the tent and in the beam of my flashlight saw the contents of our snack bags strewn over the ground, and we heard more noises in the bushes behind us. I stepped out of the tent and shined my light to where the noise was coming from, and I saw a big, black hunk with two shiny eyes. Black bear? Oh no! Pete jumped out of the tent and saw what I saw, and we pushed the boat back into the water and got in, sat down, and with the light we saw the black thing – definitely a bear, no doubt!

We decided to leave our stuff for the bear and come back in the morning for our tent and the leftovers scattered about. So, we started the motor and drove right to the city park by the beach. We walked back toward the highway and found a lawn spot to lay down on, to sleep. We lay down there and in fifteen minutes or so, we heard noises behind us. We both stood up and there, at a park trash can, was another bear pulling stuff out of the can. We ran back to the boat, put our light jackets on, and left the park. We walked to my house and slept on the floor in the front porch, saying we would go back to the boat and get our stuff from the beach tomorrow. "Tonight is a night for the bears!"

MARCH BLIZZARD - 1958

At 7:30 AM one morning, our good friend, Melvin Scott, drove Gary and me to the small gravel pit where the trail began leading into the forest. We were challenging an upcoming blizzard from Canada to find out if two beaver dams, four miles off of the highway, were active with beavers. We had our plan in place, and if the blizzard actually struck us, we were going to sleep overnight on the trail and Melvin was to pick us up at 8 o'clock the next morning.

We were confident though, that we could get back to the highway before dark and catch a car ride back to town, so Melvin knew if we didn't show up at his house at a reasonable time that evening, we would be settled down for the night in the shelter we carried.

We had packed our gear, anticipating the worst-case overnight event, and Melvin questioned us thoroughly regarding the details of our preparations. We wore our long johns, heavy wool breeches and warm wool socks, but the small stuff was also important. Our packs contained a hatchet, one pint of fuel oil, sleeping bags, food, one folding camp shovel, canteens, spare socks, and canvas with hardware to set up a shelter.

Even though we satisfied his questions, Melvin seemed a bit worried and expressed his concern. We agreed that if visibility became a significant problem, the best place to hole up for the night would be several miles east of the highway where Melvin left us. The bluff was prominent with a sheer face that rose up about fifty feet above the trail. At the top of the bluff, a narrow pine ridgeline formed and continued northerly, sloping gently down through birch and poplar trees to the first beaver dam. The base of the bluff with its dense pine ridge on top provided a good windbreak and campsite location.

We knew of the blizzard warnings but, having experienced early spring storms in the past, Gary and I decided we were well prepared to make the trip. The snow covered the ground on the four-mile trek to the bluff, which was a mile or so from the first beaver dam, and the 6 to 8-inch ground cover made for slightly slower progress than we had anticipated, our snowshoes sinking enough to cause a mild-but-tiresome drag on our legs.

I was sixteen years old at the time, and Gary was fourteen. I had been trapping for three years and had some muscle structure resulting from tramping the forests, streams and lakeshores during the frozen winter season, so I stayed in the lead, breaking trail to make it easier for Gary. He and I had previously decided to go on this jaunt to see if there were any beaver colonies active in the dams. Gary hadn't done any trapping and didn't plan to start, but he liked to hunt, fish, and tramp through the woods, as we had done many times in the past couple of years. On the other hand, Pete and I had much successful experience and had earned enough spending money to keep us actively involved in trapping and selling pelts. Pete and I had learned much of the detail from his cousin Skip, and by virtue of some good luck and a lot of hard work, we became quite proficient. This short trip with Gary was to determine if the beaver at this dam were active, giving Pete and I new territory to add to our growing trap lines.

When we reached the campsite at the base of the bluff, we took off our backpacks and immediately began to chop off the dry wood from downed trees and set up the shelter against the bluff wall. Our shelter was composed of sheets of canvas propped up by poles we created from the dry wood, which we set up with its back up to the bluff. We staked it down around the canvas perimeter on both the inside and outside ground flaps. On the outside we placed thick limbs on top of the canvas flap which we covered and packed with snow on top, to create a barrier for snow and wind. We filled the inside shelter floor with pine boughs and a canvas cover on top, and we laid the sleeping bags out over them.

The essential wood and rocks were piled in two stacks next to the fire pit (batch one and batch two). We filled the bottom of the existing fire pit with small, dry, dead branches, then added larger wood stacked on top of that. Over the top we laid five-foot long, six-inch diameter birch wood that extended over the ends, so as to burn the birch in half. We then sprinkled several ounces of fuel oil in the heart of the pile and on the larger wood in the center and lit the bottom. In ten minutes, we had a flaming fire that was flapping around the stacked rocks (the source of the rocks at the base of the bluff was more than adequate for our needs).

Leaving the fire to heat the rocks we had placed around it, we trekked as fast as possible up the east side of the pine ridge trail and down the slight slope to the first beaver dam, one mile away. It was a slightly grown over, upward rising trail that bore down to lower ground closer to the beaver dam. As we walked, the wind picked up from near northerly as a light snowfall became progressively more horizontal.

By the time Gary and I got to the first dam, the snowfall had become more intense and the wind had increased considerably. An initial look at the dam quickly answered our first question, as the structure had been blown wide open, probably by dynamite from an upset neighbor, and the pond area was empty save for the trickle of a small stream. With no sign of beaver, we knew there was no reason to check the second dam, and with the deteriorating weather, it became obvious that we needed to get back promptly to the bluff. I was familiar with the lay of the land and had taken several compass readings after leaving the bluff, so I had a good idea of the terrain in memory and was confident that we could backtrack to the bluff without delay.

We turned and started back at a moderately fast pace, following our original tracks, but soon became aware that the blowing snow was rapidly reducing our visibility and filling in our tracks. I picked up the pace and told Gary that we needed to jog as much as we could to make the best use of what tracks remained. Gary, lacking the practice required to jog with snow shoes, was finding it difficult to maintain an adequate pace. Our somewhat increased pace helped for a while, but as minutes passed, only faint depressions of the disappearing tracks were visible; about five minutes later, they were gone, and our visibility deteriorated to short bursts of fifty feet or less intermingled with fifteen to twenty seconds of whiteout! Having nearly a mile ahead of us, I began to have the sinking feeling that a poor decision had been made.

I had been depending on the compass to get us close enough for visual sighting and recognition of the ridge line, but reality struck a blow when the periods of visibility dropped close to zero and I could no longer see the compass needle for the snow! The visibility and stability of the compass in the thick wind-driven snow was making readings nearly impossible, and the plummeting temperature began to numb my fingers while holding the brass frame, trying to shield the compass face with the other hand. I soon realized we were facing unexpected physical limitations in a storm situation we had never previously experienced, and still so far away from shelter.

After several minutes of dealing with my concealed panic from not yet being at our camp site at the pine ridge, I continued trying to brush the snow off of the compass while positioning myself with my back to the wind. When again this failed, I unzipped my outer jacket down a foot or so and pulled it up, allowing me to tuck my head into the opening. Holding the compass about a foot lower, down inside the open flap, I was able to see short glimpses of the needle. Repeating this every forty to fifty seconds, we were able to continue in the right direction. I felt that another ten minutes or so would put us into the pines on the ridge, but I also was aware that our slowing pace was altering that time. Knowing that our course had to be very close to SW, my greatest concern was missing the pines by being just slightly to the east of the narrow ridge where the elevation dropped off, and the slight uphill to the SW, being not detectable, would have us pass right by the pines without seeing them.

The dropping temperature and slightly damp clothing added to our discomfort, with our hands and feet becoming more uncomfortable, and having to open my jacket frequently to verify direction was becoming a significant problem. Fatigue had set in and as much as we did not want to stop, we needed to rest. We paused, and I reassured Gary that we were still on the right course to be in the pines shortly.

After a short rest, we slowly trudged along while the visibility progressively deteriorated to the point of whiteout and the frequency of compass verifications was diminishing. I fought off the panic-stricken thought that it was no longer possible to detect the slight uphill slope which would lead to the pine ridge bluff, the location of our shelter and provisions. I made a short correction to take us a little more to the west in our direction of travel, to ease my mind a bit. If we missed the slope, we would also miss the ridge and the bluff without knowing upon which side of the ridge we were walking. Missing either way would require a lengthy and time-consuming search period.

Perhaps it would be possible to make the three miles back to the highway…

I had decided not to show my concern to Gary, as I could tell he certainly had some concern of his own. Then, a very short time after I thought it was likely that we missed the pine ridge, in a brief moment of slight calm in the wind, through the haze of the wafting snow, the shape of pine trees dimly appeared, not far away, to our right front. With my arm extended toward the tree, I shouted back to Gary "LOOK!"

As he caught up with me, I could see the smile on his face. I smiled, too, while I contemplated the next obstacle to face and problem to solve.

Under the cover of the pine trees, the visibility improved somewhat, and we knew that staying on the ridge would take us right to the bluff and our provisions. We wound our way around the east side of the bluff and back to our camp site.

When we had originally set up camp, we set enough rocks in and around the pit to line the inside of the shelter and our sleeping bags. Now we tested the rocks to see if they would sizzle when drops of snow contacted them. When they did, it was time to place them inside the shelter perimeter and the sleeping bags. With the camping shovel and heavy gloves on hands, we transferred the largest to the insides of the shelter and the smaller to the inside of the sleeping bags. We laced the door flap closed and got into our sleeping bags and felt the comfort of the heat and wondered just how long they would stay warm. Comfortable now, we pulled our very cold sandwiches and canteens of water from our back packs and enjoyed our supper. Sitting safely inside the shelter, we could now talk about our adventure.

At 5:30 PM, I gave Gary my top layer jacket and put on the raincoat from my backpack. I checked the fire pit and added the second batch of firewood.

Soon the time was 7 PM and the wind was still blowing. I peeked out the flap and saw the wood was about half consumed. We concluded that we should zip up in the bags and put the army blanket over the both of us and get some sleep. About 2 AM, I woke up and talked with Gary who said he was doing good. He told me that he renamed his sleeping bag "the imagination bag marvel" because it felt as if it wasn't even there. However, the rocks were still slightly warm, and he was going back to sleep. We laughed and decided 6 AM would be our wakeup time.

At 6 AM, we put our warm, dry socks on, slipped our feet into our boots, and climbed outside. There was about a foot of snow on the ground, but the wind was still. We quickly dismantled the shelter and repacked our belongings. The fire was out. We shook the snow off of our snow shoes and slipped our boots into them, making haste as we moved west, toward the highway. We got to the road at about 7:45 AM and Melvin was already there with a big smile on his face and a loud greeting of happiness when we told him how well our night went!

THE ICE RAFT

One early spring, several boys from Orr got together at the Sucker Creek outlet railroad bridge and had the dandy idea to take some disposed-of railroad ties and bind them together, to form a raft upon which they would pole their way to drift downstream into the Pelican eastside bay.

They designed and built that dandy raft and climbed aboard, and sure enough, the creek flow floated them about 40 yards down the creek and through the bog, with little poling effort needed to get them into the mouth of the open bay water. Once into the open water, floating into the bay, they quickly realized they had to start heading to shore, choosing Hobo Point as their destination. As they changed direction, they poled into the ice which covered the shoreline and realized they would have to break ice alongside and in front of the raft.

Beating the ice into pieces while continuing to keep the raft level was the only way to proceed to their destination, and slowly but surely, they continued to smash the ice in front of them along the 80 yards of boggy shoreline. But the ice they broke in the front continued to be in their way as they moved forward; the boggy lakeshore kept the freed ice pieces from floating around to the rear of the raft. They continued to hammer the ice but were hardly moving as they got into the last stretch, approaching Hobo Point. Finally, several fellows on land heard them and saw their dilemma, tossed them a rope, and pulled the raft toward shore. At the point the raft could move no further, the shivering cold riders got off into the icy, waist deep water and stumbled the last 50 feet to land. Our boys did good, especially when they stumbled that last fifty feet in the dark! Good job, boys!

Thanks to the fellow helpers on the shore!

DOLLY'S QUESTION

I said to Dolly, "I will soon have the story to tell on paper."

Dolly said, "I am anxious to read the whole story. You had more guts than I had. I really wanted to go to business school in the cities after graduation, but I didn't have the money or the guts to leave Orr and go. I often look back and wish I had. I wanted no loans, so I got married instead. It was an okay choice and I would take the same path again or, to be smarter, I'd take both paths. So, whatever motivated you to go in so many different and interesting directions in the first place?"

I said, "Incentives; the answer was easy because we had the opportunity to learn new things to do." Actually, I think because Pete and I had so many interests to capture our time and limited funds, it was inevitable that I always had a plan of action, leading me to learn things I didn't understand. For me, it started at an early age, making trips with Steve Gheen, flying to border lakes, delivering supplies to guys on fishing expeditions. I had been doing a lot of things by myself as a preference, and when Steve saw that, my flying lessons began. Successive interests took me to various new territories, and I followed whichever interest tugged the most. Ron got me going into radio, TV and electronics, and because my father also repaired them and was a ham operator for a number of years, I learned the fundamentals by exposure and osmosis. My father didn't like me using his equipment, but when he was gone on his trips to Duluth to haul merchandise back to the store, I spent time at his work bench in the back room of the store, and after many hours previously watching what he did and how the equipment was used, I discovered I knew what I was doing. Later on, in physics class, I really took an interest in electronics theories and understood the concepts well. Then, with Pete and me trapping for four winters, we took on definite learning experiences that led to other things. Any new experience or environment pulled us into learning new things, so I just let my interest lead in whatever direction gave me new options. Until age 15, we hitchhiked a lot to movies, to buy school clothes and to visit friends.

Another aspect, during the school years, was living with other families. I learned a lot from the Agnews, Applebys, Holmans, Hoffers, Lammis, Scotts and Siiros. Gordon Holman had me driving the flatbed truck so he could load and stack hay bales when I was 13, and Gordon's brother Bob had me learning guitar chords, something that from six years old I had wanted to learn. Prior to that, I had worked with Burt, Jim and Bob for a whole summer in the woods, peeling pulp, and then Jim and Gordon showed me how to use the cutting torch at the junk yard to cut screws which held field coils in starters and generators, separating the iron from the copper. I learned a lot of mechanic tasks and made many trips with Gordon to Duluth in the truck that hauled crushed auto bodies and scrap metals to recycle. I also made late night trips delivering wild rice to International Falls, helping Gordon stay awake. I learned about farming and dairy cattle from being with the Agnews for two summers and part of a school year. During the high school years we enjoyed different activities, things like boxing, table tennis, and playing pool in Lammi's basement, which we called "Lammi's Educational Center" – a warm place we could go to be active on cold winter days – and then there was Lammi's north shore cabin, where we played badminton on warm summer days.

Never a dull day did we have! So, Dolly, those were the days gone by in our world, but read on – and thanks for being an important part of holding together details of our past.

On my hitchhike trip to Phoenix I saw a plaque in a small garden plot downtown. It is a part of "God's Garden" by Dorothy Frances Gurney:

> "The kiss of the sun for pardon,
>
> The song of the birds for mirth,
>
> One is nearer God's heart in a garden
>
> Than anywhere else on earth."

Thank you, Dorothy, and thank you, Dolly.

SUCKER CREEK SKIP DAY

During the first week of spawning in Sucker Creek, the croppies and suckers would gather around and between medium-sized boulders in the creek and you could slowly dip your hands around their bellies and squeeze, flipping them onto the creek bank for cleaning and processing. On the selected day, the males in upper classes declared a skip day where they all gathered at the creek under the old Highway 53 road bridge and began to pick out fish in the rocks. Two classmates set up shop to clean the fish. Other fellows would uncover an old washtub and fill it with firewood and smaller wood sticks, then pack leaves and dry branches into it and start a red-hot fire. Once the fire was burned down and red cinders remained, moss was added to the top to set the fish onto, for roasting. In an hour or so, the fish would be removed and placed on paper plates for all to eat. That was our "legal" skip day. Good times, again!

On the following week-end day, many men had a choice of catching suckers in either Sucker Creek or Elbow Creek, which was always packed with suckers, even more so than Sucker Creek. There, the manpower was one man in the creek and a second man on the bank holding a potato (gunny) sack. When the man in the creek threw the suckers on the bank, the other would fill the sack. It was typical to fill several sacks full out of Elbow Creek, and there was no limit. When the men were done filling the sacks with fish, they would take them home, clean and filet them, and set them into a wash tub filled with a brine of salt, brown sugar and water. The fish would stay in the brine for four to five days, being moved around in the brine to keep it circulating. After the five days, they would place the fish in a smoke house for another two to three days until roasted.

Most smoke houses were made from old refrigerators. An exhaust hole was drilled in the top for a small amount of the smoke and heat to circulate and exit. The heat was from an electric hot plate upon which sat a metal oven pan, filled with chips of birch wood. We processed enough smoked fish to last most of the summer and well into the winter, packed in milk cartons and frozen solid in the freezer with water, to be thawed out as needed. Good stuff!

JUDY – GONE!

Until I met Judy, I believed life was always conflict, but she led me in a new direction. Perhaps it saved my life, or perhaps she pulled me up from the lowest point of my life. She and I met a year before her family moved closer, if forty-two miles away could be called "close," to Orr School. Our parents were having a meeting regarding the status of our grocery store and we kids were outside in the cold, waiting for the meeting to end. I will always remember her face when that cold wind gave her the shivers, and although it was a short meeting, I saw enough to know there was mystery in her eyes. I was about sixteen years old at the time, and it was the lack of self-image and age that had me questioning "who am I?" – a point I would return to sooner than I knew. Judy and her older brother came to our school when she was entering eleventh grade; Orr School was the twelfth school she had attended in the past eleven years. This sad fact often kept the smile from glowing on her face, and it became my duty to make the smile-side visible. She never had a social life in school, so I made a space in our social life for her to join, and that she did. We had no conflicts and were happy in the halls. After we began to go to movies together, a mutual respect and attraction became more meaningful and we wanted it to continue forever. "No conflict" were our passwords to the smiles we shared and we were more than friends, less than lovers.

I had few good feelings about my jobs, but Judy spoke much about how I was smart enough to do well and would be able to find good jobs, which was a self-image booster for me, even though I lacked credentials. I often dreamed about being a pilot, teacher, engineer, or having other high-level positions requiring higher education – much of which I lacked – but her continuing confidence prompted my mind to believe it was attainable.

The end of that school year shattered our very pleasant life, when Judy's family moved back to Arizona where her father had connections with jobbers.

On our last summer day together we shared many wishes about what and where the future would take us, and we vowed to write letters often and make plans for the next summer, after my high school graduation, when I would travel to Arizona for a get-together, to take in a few movies and walks around town.

I watched as their vehicles and trailer slowly passed through the town and sadness was plentiful in my mind. We talked on the phone for a full school year, and she wanted to see me again, so I said I would come to Phoenix after graduation. In the meantime, a situation brewed a barrier where I was either rooked or rocked with lies told by classmates to Judy about me, which served to create a shell around her, but she still wanted me to come to Phoenix. Every thought in my mind knew it was the end of our days.

My senior year in school was a total change for me as I blocked as many memories as possible and spent all my spare time working on my studies, raising my grades, and communicating with teachers regarding plans for future education and vocations.

At 7:30 PM every Friday evening I called Judy and we talked for one hour, enjoying our mutual connection and support. All went well with our plans, and we determined that I was going to leave for Arizona the week following graduation. No obstacles were in our way until a regular customer at my parent's store was stricken with cancer; he was very ill, and their daughter was sad and isolated. Out of concern for her daughter, her mother sent word through a friend, asking me if I would take her daughter to a movie – they were quite upset about her isolation and the effect it was having on their family. Even the girl's boyfriend asked me if I would help, hoping that by taking her to a movie her sad mood might be lifted, for the sake of her father's concern.

Judy had remained in touch with other classmates, and I knew that if I agreed to this arrangement someone would tell her I was dating the daughter, which would sever my position with Judy. I said "no" to the request and found myself ostracized as a result. Two days later, the daughter's friends approached me with a plan to have two couples of friends go with us to a movie, to which I again said "no," but I did agree to go with them to visit the family. When we went to their house, the ailing father, who was told that I was taking his daughter to a movie, thanked me for doing this. Because of their long history as customers at our store, I didn't have the heart to explain that I actually had said "no." Both the mother and father were quite comforted that I had agreed to this outing and would spend time with their sorrowful daughter.

The follow-up was brutal for me, as by the following Friday night Judy already knew I took the daughter to a movie. My response to her was precisely the total truth. I even wrote a letter the following week, with a repeat of the truth of the story, but this made no change in Judy's understanding of what had happened and my role in it. I apologized and asked if she still wanted me to make the trip after graduation, and she said "Yes, I still want to see you again."

After graduation, I went to the bank and took $100 from my account, knowing the trip would be somewhat more than that. I packed my small suitcase and on the following Monday I took my suitcase and to my parents said, "Goodbye, I will be back in a week or so." I crossed the railroad tracks and stood beside the highway to start showing my thumb; the third car that came by pulled over to the shoulder, stopped and told me, "Set your suitcase in back and jump in the front seat."

FROM ORR TO FARGO

To capture the attention of traffic, I wore my best-looking clothes and got rides with ease. First one – straight ride to Fargo by car with a restaurant owner from Orr. Next ride – Fargo to Sioux City. The friendly truck driver talked all the way to Sioux City and when we stopped there, he asked a waitress to please get me a ride to the Omaha bus station. Within fifteen minutes, I was in a truck on its way to Omaha. We arrived after nightfall, and the driver dropped me off at the Omaha bus station where I bought a ticket to Kansas City, to catch another night bus to Phoenix.

PARTNERSHIP AGREEMENTS

When I got on the bus in Omaha to Kansas City, I took a bench seat behind two talkative young ladies who were going to Kansas City, to stay with an aunt for a week. They began to talk with me after the bus pulled out and for an hour we chattered; they were entertained with my stories and as the night fell dark, they invited me to sit with them on their bench seat. One of them suggested I be used as a resting partner until we arrived in Kansas City, and we laughed when I asked, "Where is my place in this partnership?" The laugh clarified that my role as "head resting device" was it! After a half hour or more, they had me add more stories. When darkness was full set in, the girl on my left used my shoulder for a pillow and the girl on the right used my leg for a pillow, and within ten minutes they were both sleeping – all the way to Kansas City.

At Kansas City we got off the bus and said goodbyes and "Thanks, pardners." Laughing, I said, "A long ride is ahead of me, pardners. Now I can sleep for several hours!" I walked with them to their aunt's car, said my final vaya con dios, and went inside.

I bought my ticket to Phoenix and laid down on one of the hard benches inside, dozing off for a half hour until it was time to get on the bus. I went directly to the back bench seat and because the bus wasn't full, I did get the sleep I needed.

I awoke to loud voices and saw several people clustered at the middle of the bus, and by the road signs saw that we were heading south. I knew the bus was on highway 25 and that we would eventually be heading west, but when a couple hours later I saw a road sign saying Las Vegas 75 miles, I was very confused. My mind was trying to figure it out and eventually I came to realize this was a different Vegas, not the one in Nevada. Soon after, the names of cities on signs helped me to recognize that we were coming up on highway 40 west.

The rest of the trip went by fast, seeing new things along the way and stopping at several bus stops. Judging by our speed and location, we were still another night from Phoenix and I was a bit concerned, as I had figured it would be daylight when we arrived. There would be another night of driving down from Flagstaff, through a significant twisting, turning, route - still a long way to Phoenix. Many more miles lay ahead of us, through Sedona, Cottonwood, Prescott and across to Cordes Junction; another night coming up. I wasn't wrong a bit, but good thing I was on a bus! The canyon was a sweat. The route was terrible, and we had a lady on board with a child who was not handling it well. The twisting, turning, ups and downs, corners and curves – the only way you could see if cars were coming was by turning off the headlights to see other's oncoming lights around the curves. With the crying child, the driver was going bats so much that he stopped once and shouted, "Lady, shut that kid up or we will need to put you off at the next roadway for safety, and for God's sake!"

Surprisingly, after his outburst there were a few moments of silence with beeps in between, but with volume below the previous level.

We finally made our way out of that curvy road and arrived at Camp Verde, and in another hour or so, we made it to Payson. It was hard to believe all of that was necessary, and it was still going to take two hours. Was I ever wrong in estimating the time it would take to arrive in Phoenix!

It was no wonder everyone, including Judy's father, was chewing bitters in my name by the time I arrived. I could never have foreseen all of this, nor could I blame them at all one bit for being frustrated at my lack of timing. I was a bumpkin, definitely all the way out of my mind's senses, next to dumb at best. I worked out the return trip much better, avoiding buses that have no written schedules, but in those days we couldn't expect much more, and I guess I fit in rather well!

By night's end, day three, we pulled into a stop at the Phoenix bus station. True to my curious nature, I went outside to examine the heat; the traffic was busy! I had never seen so many cars going back and forth, horns blowing, fists waving and people shouting; I ignored it all and kept walking, not knowing where I was going, until I finally turned and made it back to the bus station to find Judy's father sitting there waiting for me, chewing me out for not calling and not waiting. He was right, but after three days on the road I needed to move, as I usually do after long trips. Every day I go bonkers if I don't get my three-mile hike and workout.

The three days in the Phoenix heat were educational. Judy was not the same person she was; in just one year we both were more alert and had lost much of our humor, becoming like strangers again.

I was hoping to see more of the girl she was, but signs and friendly smiles had diminished, and I sensed my being there was as a stranger. Something else in her life had cancelled our chances of having a future together; for us to be compatible. This was validated when she told me that a neighbor lady friend from across the street wanted to talk (to tell me that I was being politely rejected, as I had expected). There never was a chance of future before I made the trip, yet the feeling of appreciation is never forgotten.

The neighbor drove the message home and said I would be going to the bus station in the morning, that Judy was not going to be my wife. She said, "You look good, smart and will someday in the near future find your partner for life and will know it well at first sight! Enjoy your life and keep doing the best you can at school and you will do well!"

The next morning was quiet, except her father saying, "I will be waiting for your ride to the bus station in ten minutes." A short good-bye with Judy and we were on the road to the bus station. A cool exit expected!

The ride was quiet for fifteen minutes and at the station we sat in the car, and he gave me a twenty-dollar bill for food along the way home and said, "Good luck!" I responded with "Thank you, Neil, and give my thanks to your daughter."

I bought a ticket for Reno, where I would leave the bus and begin my hitchhike home.

I got on the bus and a young lady with a five-year old brother invited me to sit with them, so I did. It was comfortable and relaxing, time to reset my woes, and she offered me a job with her father's hardware store – he was looking for help. I turned down the offer and explained I was enrolled in college for the next four years (which actually lasted six years, including my master's degree). Before the bus was ready to leave Reno, with a bit of sorrow still left in my mind, I said good-bye, shook hands with the little brother and exited the bus. I took out my map and traced the road to Redmond, Oregon and walked towards the edge of town, where one car picked me up in the right direction. On the road heading north, I was picked up by a fellow who smelled a bit of alcohol and offered me a drink, which I turned down. He happily offered a ride to Redmond, as he was on his way home, too. I kept him awake and he thanked me when he dropped me off at a small hotel, and early next morning I took a small bus on a short drive to an aviary park outside of town.

At the park were many beautiful peacocks, some grouse, partridge, and a swarm of redwing blackbirds which despised my in-style white jacket with a black collar. It was the black color that they dived at and squawked about terribly, nearly landing on my head! Even the blackbirds wanted me to go home.

I got back on the road, and with six or seven rides I was left off at Idaho Falls. The end of the day was approaching and I needed a bed for the night, so I walked the main street and saw a hardware store and went inside and asked the man, "Is there a place I can find a room for the night?" His answer was, "You know, I have my mother close by so let's see what she says." On the drive, he told me she had a big house with spare rooms, and upon arrival she shared a big smile and said "Of course, and it comes with breakfast at 8:30 AM." After dinner, we talked about my trip and I told her the story, then a full night's sleep was made great with a better breakfast!

By the time I reached the Yellowstone west gate on the second day, I had spent too much time in Redmond, so it was late in the afternoon. I saw Old Faithful again (the first time was in 1952), and had a bite to eat, then decided to hit the road. I became aware, as I walked to the main highway, that there were very few cars in the lot or on the road, but I was rather confident that I would get a ride. The distance from there to Gardiner, Montana was about 15 miles, and too quickly it began to get dark. About a half hour later, I worried a bit, as there had been only a couple of cars that went by. In the middle of Yellowstone Park, where the bears and the buffalo roam, I started to feel the evening chill.

Another ten minutes went by and I finally saw car lights in the distance! Hooray! They didn't stop. I watched them as they continued onward down the hill, then I saw the brake lights come on as they pulled over to the side of the road. A woman took one step outside of the car, then got back in, leaving me disappointed as they pulled back onto the road; but then, about twenty yards further down, they stopped again and began to back up. They slowly backed toward me, and as they finally got to where I was standing, the lady, about seventy-some, opened her car door and peeked out at me and said, "Do you have a gun?"

My "certainly not" didn't seem to convince her, so she asked, "A knife then?" In the most pleasant voice I could muster, I said, "You folks are the only people I have seen for the past 2 1/2 hours, and if I am to be out here for the rest of the night with only the wolves and the bears, I may not live to see the bright of tomorrow; so if I had a gun or a knife, I would quickly throw it away and beg you for a ride down the hill to Gardiner!" That put a smile on her face and she said, "Son, you are dressed nicely and speak well, so please get in the back seat and tell us why you are hitch hiking in the dark to Gardiner," so I hopped in and told them my story on the twenty minute drive.

As I was getting out in Gardiner, I thanked them very much, and she turned and looked at me and said, "Thank you for the tantalizing story, and God bless you with a long and fruitful life, and thanks for not harming us!"

There were a lot of stories made along the trip, and I was left with the lesson that this country is full of nice people, but not many of them pick up hitch hikers after dark.

I walked down to the river to spend the night sleeping under the bridge where the sound of the water beckoned, but the thick humidity felt too cold, so I walked several blocks northwest of town and spent that cold night sleeping behind a church, on the sidewalk leading to the back door. It was cold, and I had only a light jacket, and a couple of spare shirts and jeans, so I shivered much of the night, and as I watched the bright Sputnik reflection moving through the background of stars, I thanked God for getting me to Gardiner, Montana!

When the morning light of dawn became apparent in the sky, I took off my extra pair of jeans and put them in my suitcase and walked out to the street. The traffic was scant, so I continued to walk to the outer limits of the city. Several cars passed by. It was a little warmer than the night, and as I walked I felt better knowing that a ride was coming my way and the day had begun; a feeling of relief fell over me.

The next four cars went by and several minutes later, a yellow Volkswagen pulled over and waved me in. "How far you going this morning?" the smiling young man asked. I responded with a smile, saying "Hope you're heading towards Fargo!" "Well, I can get you as far as Billings this morning, but I'm heading north to Canada from there." "That sounds great!" I replied.

The ride felt great now that there was heat involved, and it wasn't very long before my head slid against the window and I dozed off. About twenty minutes later I heard something hit the roof and my eyes snapped open about the same time as Ken applied the brakes and pulled over to the side of the road. We sat and chatted a bit as the light hail bounced off the car, with several marble-sized ones causing a little concern to Ken. Fifteen or twenty minutes later it quit and we started off again, but just a few miles east of Livingston very large hailstones, like I had never seen before, filled the ditches on both sides of the road. Several cars were parked along the road with damaged windows and dents where the large hail had hit. Ken told me to take another snooze if I wanted, so I did for over a half hour, then talked with him for the next hour before we arrived in Billings. I thanked him as I got out on the east side, and he wished me good luck and drove off. It was still mid-morning and I walked and thumbed as I walked. It wasn't long before a car beeped and pulled over to the street side where all four fellows bailed out and stretched a bit while I gave them my story and introduction. They were very polite and gave me room in the back seat on the driver's side; a tight fit, but no complaints.

Around noon, we stopped for a sandwich in Bismarck and they paid for mine, with many thanks to each, then we were on our way to Duluth, Minnesota. The guys were headed east and north of Duluth on a fishing trip at the inland lakes that provide for a nice catch. They dropped me off at the bus station and each handed me a five-dollar bill. With my huge thanks for such a gift for the bus fare, I bought my ticket, got off at Virginia, walked north, and caught a ride to Orr, my home. After a nice night's rest, the next day I told my story to Mom who said "there are lots of fish in the ocean and sand in the sea" and that neighbor was correct, "now that you've arrived at home, that grain of sand should be showing up soon."

The following week I talked with friends and gave short stories to the restaurant gangs, and I let them know I would be registering at the two-year community college in Virginia, which is exactly what I did.

Before I left for Phoenix I had talked to Tim, who also played guitar; we had good times with rock and boogie guitar music, and we spent much of the next two years playing the homemade music of our duo, "the RAB2." I aspired to studying pre-med, but the cost of the education bumped me out. I continued to follow my interest, though, by reading research studies in medical innovations, still hopeful that this might be my path. As time went by, however, the reality of the finances sent me in a different direction.

My wife, Bea, happened upon the scene and helped me pay through six post-secondary years of high-level college and eighteen months of electrical control systems, design and developing to replace outdated, obsolete electrical circuitry and electronic designs. I taught six years of heavy duty electrical and mechanical maintenance and three and a half years of electronic equipment, and I passed all requirements to get my pilot's license.

I had a straight arrow in my desires and made those targets my goals, hitting a bulls eye each and every time. Learning was my desire. My wife and children became my satisfaction and we have helped all of our family attain their goals throughout the years, including top diplomas in education, mathematics, engineering, and degrees up through PhDs.

Judy was a part of the spark that set my goals high, and my wife Bea carried the spark to high flame when I reached the top electrical engineering position in the 1970's. My life has been full of blessings in many ways, and the stories I tell sent sparks flying – sparks that grew brighter and created the momentum to carry them to the finish. A number of times, help was needed from a higher level, help that I desperately needed to intercede at just the right moments. Thank you, God, for the gift of your vision.

SUMMER HARVEST OF 1963

My summer of 1963 was motivating. I finished my first quarter at UMD Duluth, and during my final tests I had a significant pain attack at work, and the first quarter was next to being shot. The grades were not the worst, but the appendix operation set me back when my insurance paid less than I anticipated. A friend of mine with whom I had roomed at the two-year college in Virginia moved to Minneapolis, so I decided to take some classes in Minneapolis and moved in with my friend, Gene.

As the spring quarter college days went by, I needed a job. A friend told me about how many workers were needed for the summer harvest and that he had connections if I was interested, so he set it up for me and I drove to Oklahoma. My first task was to plow fields for a farmer for two weeks, after which I could join a combine group that traveled from Texas to Canada, harvesting grains of several different kinds: Wheat, corn, flax and barley. After my plowing job was over, I joined the harvest group and we began the trip, with our first job harvesting corn at a fellow's farm who was providing one combine and a haul truck for the summer.

We had a good bunch of workers, and I was to operate a combine and at times would drive grain haul trucks to nearby storage silos.

We continued moving along at the speed of the ripening of the various grains, sometimes fast and sometimes slow. Regardless, it was a good time, seeing what the country's states are like.

Our jobs in the Phillipsburg area were good, with the wheat being thick yield, so much that at the end of one day, the owner told us to work until midnight as fast as we could, in a race to beat the rain forecast for tomorrow. Early that next morning, there was no rain and we had one large load of wheat to deliver to the silo. Our elderly combine owner said he would take the truck there. I asked him if he would like me to drive it instead, and he said, "That would be fine, Ray, thank you."

I got a good start and drove the straight road to town. A portion of the road, about half the way to town, had a one-mile wide dry wash with only one lane of elevated gravel road surface across the wash. At about 80 yards across, I saw a whirlwind-like cloud coming straight at me – very fast. Several seconds later I recognized that the cloud was dust being kicked up by a vehicle, and the driver of the vehicle was driving into the morning sun. The thought struck me like lightning that he had no idea I was on the road heading towards him.

I searched my mind for options and quickly came up with several: 1) cut my speed down to 35 and set the passenger side tires on the soft shoulder and wait to see if he was going to stop (he didn't!); 2) Quickly stop and set the brakes and let him hit my truck: not good, as he would not survive the crash; 3) Back the truck up: too late and not possible without driving off the road; 4) Leave my speed at 35 and set the passenger tires onto the soft shoulder, and when he gets close enough, roll the truck upside down and make a soft landing on the cab roof and the box walls, and get some cushion from the load of wheat. Option 4 seemed the most viable to the situation.

It played out as I planned, so when he was about sixty feet in front of me and rapidly closing in, I tightly grabbed the steering wheel (to keep from flying around in the cab) and turned it moderately fast to drop the two wheels off the shoulder, causing my side of the truck to rise up into the air as the shoulder side dropped toward the bottom of the dry wash. As the driver got real, real close, it was strange looking down at him and he looking up at me through his windshield, directly into my eyes. His eyes were wide open and the look on his face was one of surprise mixed with fear as he passed by me, underneath the left side of my truck. No physical contact was made between the vehicles, but my truck roof hit the bottom of the dry wash with a mild crashing sound and the passenger side window glass breaking, the roof of the cab and the sideboards of the truck box caving in, dropping the full load of wheat which acted as a weak shock absorber for the whole truck.

My head bumped the cab roof and my tight grip on the steering wheel kept me in place rather than bouncing me around the cab, and the impact was a bit less than I had anticipated. I opened the passenger side door, crawled out and went up the bank to see the vehicle tooling away rapidly, several hundred yards down the road.

After he was out of sight, I walked to a house about a hundred yards back and the owner offered me a chair until the sheriff arrived on the scene. The sheriff drove me to the local hospital where they examined me fully for concussion, and I checked out okay! Insurance covered all of the truck damage, which was minor, and the vehicle driver received a minor ticket. Another safety lesson for one-lane roads: Find a different route!

I FOUND MY LADY - 1964

When I left Orr in 1960 after my hitchhike back from Phoenix, I packed my suitcase and got a ride with my father to Virginia, Minnesota to attend the two-year college.

While I was there, I first roomed with an Orr friend who was in his second year. He helped me with the tough math classes that year, as he was a wise fellow with a good background in it all. I missed him when we got into the more advanced classes, but my grades were adequate. The easy class was choir, so I did good there (aced that), and I met some more fellows who had a study group that I attended, which helped.

JEFF HANSON AND RAY PERFORMING AT VIRGINIA
JUNIOR COLLEGE

One of the choir group guys, Gene, and I became friends in that first year. Gene's voice was loud and mine soft, but I could more easily carry a tune, so I sang into his ear and he projected the sound loud enough for both of us. We rented a small, low priced apartment in the second year. He had a two-and-a-half-gallon milk can he filled at a neighbor's farm each week, jokingly referred to as " tubercular milk," as the farmer had once had TB. So, we ate cereal and drank fresh milk right from the cows. Actually, we had hard boiled eggs for a few mornings each week and we thrived! When Gene invited me to his house the first time, I had a good time talking with his mother, father and a smiling younger, bright fourteen year-old sister, whose name was Beatrice (Bea).

The third year, Gene moved to Minneapolis where he rented a small apartment close to the University while the rest of his family moved from near Tower, Minnesota to downtown Minneapolis when Gene's father took a night job in the city. I moved to Duluth, to attend the University of Minnesota at Duluth (UMD), and after I had appendix surgery, which decimated my fall quarter at school, I healed up and moved to Minneapolis where I roomed with Gene again. I spent the following summer working with a combine team, harvesting grains from Texas to Canada, then headed back to Minneapolis where I would be rooming with Gene again.

In the beginning of 1964, Gene invited Bea and her friend, Sandy, to our apartment where we had a surprise party for Sandy's 19th birthday. Midway through the evening, there was a knock on the door and Gene's basketball buddies were there to pick him up. Evidently, he'd forgotten the plan, so he asked me to "Take the girls home" and left me to do the entertaining. It was there that I discovered Bea was definitely a likeable lady; her wit was contagious and as a result, we caught the love bug for sure! We went to movies and drove around Minneapolis to the lakes, getting lost and finding our way back again. We window-shopped the downtown stores and admired their displays during the Christmas season, and we went up the Foshay Tower to plan our future life together. The Army and Vietnam interrupted these plans, but when I returned to Minneapolis, we took up where we left off. I attended school at Dunwoody Industrial and Bea worked at a bank as we began to live out our plans.

Now, here in 2018, we are back in downtown Minneapolis after finishing our move from Arizona's dry heat, where we lived for 25 years. After 52 years together, we still have more plans, so it's back to the Foshay Tower for us; no longer the tallest building, dwarfed by fifty years of progress.

VIETNAM EXPERIENCE – SIX MONTHS

This is a true account of my Vietnam experience with the 1ˢᵗ Air Cavalry, August 1965 through January 1966. That which I quote is quite precise as I have had non-stop mind-video scenes, hallucinations of death and suffering, and audio "Ruoho, help me, Ruoho" from real-time to distinct recollection, clear in my mind for over fifty years. Years that the V.A. says are "Not Service Connected." A PTSD life that began a week after arrival back home.

The timeline is not easy to follow as there is none, and sleep was any increment resembling dark and quiet, usually in segments of two to three hours. My whole training prior to Vietnam was infantry and I expected to end up on the line with a pistol and rifle, but I could hit the keys on a typewriter more accurately than I could pull a trigger; but to be correct and true, I couldn't miss any large, flying bird, namely partridge or quail, with my target rifle. So, stretch your own timeline as you listen, but don't fall asleep. If you are queasy about blood and death, you might not want to read this section; be forewarned, this has both. Children under 18 years old should not read this. If you know what napalm falling from an F-4 Phantom looks like, greetings and best wishes!

Shortly after arrival in Quy Nhon on 11 Sep 1965 and debarking on the 12th, I set out to accomplish my initial tasks that began by listing field, surgical and evacuation hospitals including number of beds, equipment, supplies and estimates of how many wounded could be processed in a 24-hour period. After charting out medical locations in II Corp Tactical Zone, I was given orders to report to the 229th Battalion where I loaded rocket pods, and at the end of the 3rd week the 229th Company Commander sent me to the First Air Cavalry Headquarters. As I was getting into the passenger seat, he said, "I don't know what the hell you do at Headquarters, but this guy Scully told me to get you over there 'Right now!'"

Early the following morning Scully and I hitched a ride to Quy Nhon and our convoy was fired on by Viet Cong mortar rounds while going through the first mountain pass. Our air escort quickly located the source and knocked out their position with only two 2 ½- ton trucks taking minor damage; they were pulled out of the convoy and towed back to base camp for repairs.

Scully and I were delayed in arriving at Quy Nhon airport, where we set up a meal pass ticket at the officer's mess and acquired a bunk location and a place to pick up my pay checks from the 85th Evacuation Hospital. We also made contact with the Air Force and the Dust-Off Helicopter group to arrange transportation to each medical facility until the secure radio/phone system installation was completed. If Air Force or Dust-Off were not available, I was to approach the Transportation Company or catch a convoy or any other vehicle on the road. I was to carry my M-16 with ammo packs at all times, as my assistance could be required on a firing line.

My weekly trips and transportation worked out well, and my weekly report with Scully at Base camp changed my orders often, keeping me informed and on the move. The morning that the secure radio system was up and running, the pilot who was taking me to Phu Cat said, "In the morning meeting it was said that this would be Ruoho's last trip by air and he was needed at the Base camp."

On our way back to Quy Nhon, the pilot received notice that there were four wounded soldiers needing to be picked up at LZ Falcon and I should be ready to provide fire line assistance; however, as we got within ten minutes from the LZ, another call to the pilot said the LZ was no longer under fire. We landed and helped the four aboard, then continued back to Quy Nhon and helped them into the ambulances to the 85th. When I got back to the hospital area, I was surprised to see the triage line with 60 wounded, so I went to question the head nurse. She told me that a Chinook dropped them off and said, "It's a stress and anxiety filled day with the doctors loaded down and moving as fast as they can, many of them working 24 hours without a rest, and the Administrator is not able to communicate. Several doctors have tried to get him to talk, but his silent trance remains."

As I started to fill out I.D. cards and make assessment records, a pilot friend of mine with a severe shoulder wound was laying on a nearby litter. When he saw me, he raised his good arm and with much effort said, "Ruoho, help me, Ruoho." I walked over, responded back and told him I was going to get a doctor involved and would be back soon. I asked the nurse if I could talk with the administrator and she said she would ask the doctors. She returned a few minutes later and told me, "They all said they doubt if it will help, but if you think you can get him out of his trance, go right ahead." I was upset and asked if there was anything we could do to help the pilot now and quietly she said, "I'm sorry Ray, but his wounds are bad, and you need to know he most likely isn't going to make it." I walked back to the pilot and told him I was going to talk to the administrator to see if we could get two of those C1-30s over here from Saigon MACV very soon. His arm went a bit limp and he said, "Thanks, Ray."

I walked over to the office and sat down in front of the admin's desk and said, "Sir, we have a line of 60 wounded with more in this last batch that are in dire need of emergency help to get us through this temporary bind, and MACV has flying birds with full surgery capability. With the new autoclaves we can save a number of wounded, but we need to move fast. Two or three more doctors can also be sent here with a full re-stock of supplies, ready for in-flight surgery. Saigon has what we need, all we need to do is ask. Our old Korean autoclaves are as fast as a model T with four flat tires. So, do you have a phone list for MACV?" Finally, his response was, "If your Division wouldn't have dropped off so many wounded at one time, we wouldn't have this problem." "You are right, sir, but we have a war taking place up there and you and I both have a problem, and it's our job to deal with it. In a few more hours hypothermia will set in, and we don't need more problems. If you have that phone list it wouldn't bother me to make those calls to get things rolling. I will be gone from here in a month and you have a career for the rest of your life. Tomorrow morning, I have to call in my morning report, and if you make those calls now, the report will be a lot better than if we don't get moving while there is still time to save some lives."

After a minute-long delay, looking at his desk, the administrator lifted his head, looked at me and firmly said, "Thank you, Ruoho! Thanks for talking me back to reality! I have really been out of it. Could you tell the head nurse to come here with two doctors, another nurse and a typist to start making up the supply lists and manifests. We need to get moving!" "Okay, Sir, Thanks. I'll get them in here right away!" (Hospital personnel were delighted when I told them the news!)

When the head nurse heard the instructions, she immediately passed the word around, and when I saw the pilot was no longer there on the litter, I asked her for his status. She said, "I'm sorry Ray, he didn't make it. There was nothing more we could do for him."

I made it back to my bunk for a short rest, and two hours later I heard the two 130's coming in. My friend across the aisle rattled my bunk and said, "You still want to see what those operating rooms look like? I have a jeep we can drive over there!" "Right, I said, let's go!"

After a short viewing of the immaculate inside of the operating room, I made it back to my bunk for two more hours of sleep, then got up and called Scully with a brief summary on our new secure phone and told him, "I'll have more detail when I get up there." Scully's response was:

"I need you up here as soon as you can and wear a clean white undershirt and clean fatigues; preferably, early tomorrow. Now you have more to hear: We'll have a Chinook arriving down there about 10:00 A.M. with 50 or more wounded. A second one will land about noon. You can start now by getting Graves Registration cranked up to help move the remaining 40 bodies. It isn't nice! Sorry about that."

*****

The first Chinook landed about 9:30 A.M. with about 45 wounded. With two ambulances, we helped transport them the short distance to the 85th. When that was accomplished, I went to Graves Registration to request several troops to help move more bodies to Graves work area. The sergeant in charge said, "That is not our job!" I walked back to the 85th and asked them the same question and got the same response, but when I told them that I couldn't hire the outside locals, they gave me one soldier and a 2 ½ ton truck to haul bodies. We drove to the airport to wait for the second Chinook.

At very near noon, the second flight arrived and the back ramp opened with a rush of smoke and the horrible smell of napalm and burning flesh. It rose from the two burning piles in the back of the Chinook, and the pilot, with a cloth held on his face, walked by the steaming blood-fog piles down to where we were standing on the tarmac, waiting for the smoke and steam to clear, and began to carry ordinance to the security taped-off area. Ten minutes or so later, we began to pull bodies off the top and pulled or carried them onto the tarmac, spraying them with a fire extinguisher. The first pilot went back out to the street for several more extinguishers, and he commandeered a jeep and driver to promptly find a couple of water buckets and more extinguishers.

My helper and I continued to drag bodies off the piles and extinguished most of the fires, and in about one hour we had dragged the last of the bodies onto the tarmac. The last corpse was tall and weighed more than 180 pounds, still smoldering from openings around the neck that we sprayed with one of the bottles, which appeared to have slowed the smoke. To raise him up to the truck platform, I started by lifting the legs while my helper started lifting from the top, but we were not able to lift him high enough to place him on it, so we lowered him, switched sides, and I took the heavier top. When we got him high enough to slide him onto the platform, I began to lose my grip, so we lowered him again as more smoke and drippings of hot napalm stuff began to flow.

We poured more water on the openings and repeated the lift, and when we got him up and started sliding him, his head began to slide off of his top vertebrae and landed directly into my arms, with his head and neck openings draining fire from his brain contents onto the back of my hands. The first pilot saw the flame and smoke from my gloves and told me they were on fire, so I promptly lowered his body to the ground while sharp pains shot from my back and radiated into my left leg and to my upper stomach area. As the head began to roll, I lined it back up with the vertebrae and pushed it back into place, after which the pilot pulled off my burning gloves and told me to sink my hands into the bucket. I did that and held them there, without feeling anything, for several minutes. I looked over at a stack of railroad ties and the pilot asked me if I could walk, so I took several steps, and with pain continuing I kept walking to the ties and sat down. The pilot sprayed more from the bottle on the head and neck openings and came over to me, looked at my hands and said, "You need to go to the 85th and have them fix up your hands where the burned holes are in your skin." Then he asked me, "Who at Graves refused to provide soldiers to load and transport bodies back to their work area? I told him, "The Sergeant."

I walked to the 85th and they put something on my hands and covered them with gauze, and several minutes after I returned pilot one returned, followed by several graves trucks carrying troops. They jumped out the back and began pulling and loading the bodies, of which six or seven had been burned badly with smoke still dispersing into the quiet air, one whose burned left shoulder had separated and was falling apart, another whose arms and legs were burned down to stumps much shorter than a normal leg and arm, and another whose arms and legs were totally burned off with only a charred torso remaining. When I asked the soldiers from Graves where the big man's head was, they said it was in the body bag, another said they were playing soccer with his head. I was angered and told them they should respect those who give their lives, as some day they might look like that or burn in hell.

As the dark of night expanded and the light plants came on, I looked toward the back of the lighted work area and on one of the gurneys where they had parked him was the pilot who had called me to help him, lying with his arm still slightly raised, and I was not able to look again.

When I saw the men several hours later, at about 2:00 A.M., the workers were mellow and had changed their attitude. At 3:00 A.M., after having documented all personnel body tags listing descriptions, probable direct causes of death, and placing all personal belonging items into provided bags, I picked up my M-16 and began to walk toward the 85th. Shortly after limping about 40 yards outside the gates,

I heard multiple, intermittent gunshots about 50 to 60 yards ahead and footsteps about ten feet behind my left side. My mind was blank – no fear, no feelings – so I turned to see who it was: It was my good friend Lee, oldest son of a Buddhist/Catholic family. Lee had been at the tarmac gate much of the day, watching me and the workers examine bodies, write up the required details and clean the bodies of the dead. He came closer and in a quiet voice said, "That was bad, real bad. Are you okay?" I replied, "I think I am, but my back still has sharp pain." Hearing a few more snapping shots from up ahead, Lee said, "Too much danger. Follow me very close!"

I followed him around several homes and a couple quonsets, and we were suddenly at the 85th security gate. I said, "Ruoho coming in." I turned to Lee and said, "Thanks for the help, friend, and be careful going home." He made a quiet reply, "No problem, I take short cut," as he bent over and slowly disappeared out of sight.

As I passed through the security gate, one of the guards cautioned me to stay in the dark and to enter the quonset from the back. No shower tonight and all lights off, of course.

I made my way to the back door and went to the foot locker, pulling out clean underwear, two clean white T shirts, fatigues, clean socks, two canteens of water, my helmet and dim flash light, which I carried out to the sink. I stripped off my contaminated fatigues, underwear, boots and socks and tossed them into the contamination barrel. I went back in and found two bottles of Jim Bean bonded – one full and one half-full – and took a swig of the half bottle. I stepped back outside and splashed water and soap on my rank, smelly hair and soaped my face and upper body, then poured the rest of the first canteen over the top of my head. I took another drink of J.B. and poured more of the water from the second canteen and the rest of the bottle over the top of my head. I dumped a good part of the second bottle of Beam over my head, face, upper and lower body and then drank the remainder. The J.B. was a bit hot on my sensitive parts and I used one T shirt to wipe myself dry from top to bottom. After the soap, rinse and drying, I heard a quiet noise behind me, but I didn't even bother to look; at this point, I could not care much what it was.

When I got up and put on my clean clothes after three hours of sleep, I walked across the ward to see some of the wounded. One of the nurses walked over to me and said, "Ray, I am sorry that I watched you clean up during the night. I hadn't meant to stop and watch, but I wanted to know that you were okay. I will buy you the next bottle of Beam. We were sorry that your friend didn't make it. We all appreciated very much what you did to help us get our hospital back in order."

After talking with most of the wounded, I gave Scully a phone call with a summary of events and told him I would have more information when I got up there that afternoon. Again, he said, "Come right to my office when you get here. We need to talk." "Okay," I said. "I'll be up there in an hour or so."

I hitched a ride with a Beaver courier and 25 minutes later I stepped into Scully's office. "How are you doing?" Scully asked. "A bit off and pain in the back, but otherwise I think I'm okay. My hands are numb and look weird, and a little shaky." Scully said, "The two pilots had a lot to say at this morning's meeting, then this afternoon the two doctors from the 85th heading to Pleiku stopped at my office to tell me that what you did yesterday changed a lot at the hospital. Without your actions, there would have been a different outcome for those who got evacuated, and those doctors said you certainly deserve a medal or two. They told me, 'He accomplished in ten minutes that which three of us couldn't do in an hour!'"

Scully then made some significant re-enlistment offers that I often think might have been a better road to travel, but I had other plans in place. I had been taking my replacement around and going through the details for three weeks, so Scully told me the replacement was ready to take over and I needed to take five days of R&R in Saigon, from where I could phone home and let my family and girlfriend know I would be back in Minneapolis in less than two weeks. Then Scully said, " You and I are going to go to morning roll call tomorrow morning, the first roll call we are having since we arrived here, and the first item of the roll call is to present you with a field (Blood Stripe) promotion to SGT E-5. Your actions have been significant and will be rewarded with the ACM (Army Commendation medal) to honor your accomplishments."

The following morning, the whole company was gathered and Scully made his speech and gave me the shirt with the stripes – clean and bright – that he had me put on. We walked slowly over to the officer's mess breakfast, and when we walked in the door, the noise level was high at every table, but as we walked to the empty table, the noise tapered down to complete silence. Scully pointed out the back chair and after several minutes, he said, "All of this silence now is to honor that which you have done in your Army experience, and everyone in this company knows the details. This is for you and the soldiers in this room, to remember those many who are no longer with us, and that you have completed an exemplary term of duty for this Division."

We went to Scully's office where he made the ultimate offer that made my body shudder. He sent me off with these parting words, "Goodbye, our companion and detail observer. Good Luck, my friend."

The thought of leaving Vietnam was starting to create an empty spot inside me, and I felt emotionally that I was going to miss the Vietnamese family that had been my social life when I had the time to stop by and visit with them. Their mother wanted me to take one or two of the children, and I promised that I would return if things had changed back at home.

14 Feb 1966, the day our plane left An Khe, Scully made another offer for me to stay in the Army, but I once more turned down a very significant offer that would have given me a new life; my dreams and commitments remained intact. The pilot left the ramp exit open, and it is the memory of the ocean, the city, Quy Nhon, mountains and vegetation that has stayed with me clearly over the years, now 50 years

ago. In very real ways, the children and the family I knew there are still a part of my life. I pine for those families who have lost their sons.

Wesley and I made a trip back there in 2010. Wes has returned every year since – he is there even now, as I write – and he will attempt to find the family; wherever they may be, I feel they are still the best of friends.

WESLEY CLOYS AND RAY IN VIETNAM IN 2010

30 KILOMETER MOUNTAIN TRAIL RUN

I have always had the need for exercise and when too long a stretch in between has been exceeded, the flag inside sends a message to "Move!" – sometimes more than anticipated. In April 2004, a friend from Sheridan, Wyoming called to inform me that there was a 30-kilometer mountain trail run to be held the following June, in the Bighorn Mountains, and he wanted me as his partner. Since I had over two months to get into shape, I agreed and set a goal of running five kilometers each day, up the steep mountain peak two miles behind our home in Tucson, Arizona. The workout was adequate to get into shape. Unfortunately, the steepness of the highest peak on the Bighorn trail was twice the steepness of my practice trail at home.

Consequently, the real peak nailed me on the trail run, and my start to finish time was four hours and thirty minutes; my legs gave out on the peak. The time was okay, but not satisfactory to me. It gave me a new bar, a new goal to meet.

Ted and I ran again in 2005. I pushed myself on the home peak practice trail and built up my hamstrings with a bit more body weight. Also, I went to Sheridan one week before the run and camped out in the mountains to adjust to the elevation and temperature. One morning, I was awakened by noises and slipped outside of the tent in time to see a mother moose and baby behind the tent. I quietly moved back into the tent and listened to them walk away. On another morning during a walk, while about 200 feet from the camp area, I saw a doe and a yearling. The doe paid me no attention as I walked toward them, but the small one was anxious and stepped behind a bush so he couldn't see me. When I got closer, he jumped straight up in the air which then caused his mother to notice, and she moved to calm him while I kept walking.

During my week in the mountains, I ran the peak trail portion four times and learned to slow down on the upslope, to keep my air supply stable, and doubled the downslope speed to better my time. Prior to the run I massaged my leg muscles, and that seemed to help. In the 2005 race I bettered my time to finish in four hours and zero minutes. A good run for a 63-year-old. The best finish times that year were in the two-hour time frame – hard to believe, but those athletes were also very young.

When I crossed the finish line, I was tired and immediately headed for the car to sit. As I sat there, rehydrating with Dr. Pepper, things around me began to disappear, to turn white, caused by lack of oxygen and excess heat. I sat in the car for about 15 to 20 minutes until the world came back into sight. I then made my way to the medical tent and got checked out. A little food and time continued to help, but I decided that it was time to hang up the racing shoes. My trail running days were behind me.

A FOGGY SIGHT... LAST WORDS

A greeting in 1966 at girlfriend Bea's parents' home was a cheerful event, followed up the next day with a three-foot blizzard after which Bea and I both landed in a soft, cold snowbank, laughing at the cold chill I had from lack of Vietnam heat to greet my return. I also picked up my guitar only to find that my fingers on both hands had no coordination, a warning that my memory no longer was intact, only many blanks in most all memory banks – a problem I have worked on for a lifetime in all aspects of my previous gifts. The guitar became a faint picture in my memory, absent for the most part, for the rest of my life. In its place was a trigger of unknown substitutes, namely words in formulas and books that drowned out nearly all memories of lost head and dark sleepless nights; fifty years of reruns now, in which I feel lost. However, my writing, thoughts and returning life are like a shadowbox reminiscent of a time when I had control, building that box of "pride," yet even there I find my memory banks look like tainted snowbanks on top of orange stuff with napalm clouds burning flesh across acres and acres of our boys, lives shattered and strewn in a bloody-fog... the dead scattering the devil's twenty-two warriors each day, with that box of memories and medals that evaporate every connected night!

And to those who still fight on the landing zone day and night, I apologize; to those with whom I share years of unwanted burdens, please stay with us this day and every day to come. Thank you for your service. You did your job well.

Ray E. Ruoho

ABOUT THIS BOOK

The proceeds from this book will go to help the Nguyen Nga Center in Quy Nhon, Vietnam. Ray and Wesley met Miss Nga in 2010 when they traveled back to Vietnam. The center helps those with special needs, especially those with physical disabilities.

Please read more about this place that works to bring about a chance for the disabled to lead "A Happy and Useful Life," the Center's motto.

http://www.nguyennga.org/en/

MISS NGA WITH A FEW STUDENTS IN 2010

Made in the USA
Lexington, KY
14 January 2019